RELIGION AND REALITY

The Avataric Great Sage,
ADI DA SAMRAJ

RELIGION
AND
REALITY

True Religion Is Not Belief in Any "God"-Idea
but the Direct Experiential Realization
of Reality <u>Itself</u>

BY
THE AVATARIC GREAT SAGE,
ADI DA SAMRAJ

THE DAWN HORSE PRESS
MIDDLETOWN, CALIFORNIA

NOTE TO THE READER

All who study the Way of Adidam or take up its practice should remember that they are responding to a Call to become responsible for themselves. They should understand that they, not Avatar Adi Da Samraj or others, are responsible for any decision they make or action they take in the course of their lives of study or practice.

The devotional, Spiritual, functional, practical, relational, and cultural practices and disciplines referred to in this book are appropriate and natural practices that are voluntarily and progressively adopted by members of the practicing congregations of Adidam (as appropriate to the personal circumstance of each individual). Although anyone may find these practices useful and beneficial, they are not presented as advice or recommendations to the general reader or to anyone who is not a member of one of the practicing congregations of Adidam. And nothing in this book is intended as a diagnosis, prescription, or recommended treatment or cure for any specific "problem", whether medical, emotional, psychological, social, or Spiritual. One should apply a particular program of treatment, prevention, cure, or general health only in consultation with a licensed physician or other qualified professional.

Religion and Reality is formally authorized for publication by the Ruchira Sannyasin Order of Adidam Ruchiradam. (The Ruchira Sannyasin Order of Adidam Ruchiradam is the senior Cultural Authority within the formal gathering of formally acknowledged devotees of the Avataric Great Sage, Adi Da Samraj.)

Produced by the Dawn Horse Press,
a division of the Avataric Pan-Communion of Adidam

International Standard Book Number: 1-57097-212-5
Library of Congress Catalog Card Number: 2006931608

THE "PERFECT KNOWLEDGE" SERIES

THE PERFECT TRADITION

✦ ✦ ✦

RELIGION AND REALITY

✦ ✦ ✦

THE LIBERATOR

✦ ✦ ✦

THE ANCIENT REALITY-TEACHINGS

✦ ✦ ✦

THE WAY OF PERFECT KNOWLEDGE

The books of the "Perfect Knowledge" Series are drawn from
*Is: The "Perfect Knowledge" of Reality and The "Radical" Way
to Realize It,* by the Avataric Great Sage, Adi Da Samraj.

The five books of the "Perfect Knowledge" Series
together comprise the complete text of *Is*.

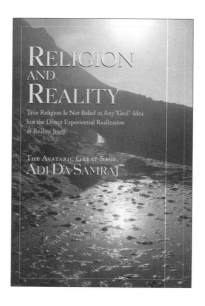

ABOUT THE COVER

Throughout His Life, Avatar Adi Da Samraj has worked to develop means—both literary and artistic—of communicating the True Nature of Reality. He approaches the creation of His literary and artistic works as a process of Revealing What Reality Is and how Its True Nature can be Realized.

For the cover of *Religion and Reality*, Avatar Adi Da has chosen a photograph He took in 1964 on the coast of Northern California.

Examples of the artwork of Adi Da Samraj, together with discussions of His artwork and His own statements about it, may be seen online at:

www.daplastique.com

CONTENTS

Introduction to *Religion and Reality*   9
by Megan Anderson, Jonathan Condit, PhD, and Carolyn Lee, PhD

RELIGION AND REALITY

Moving Beyond Childish and Adolescent Approaches   15
to Life and Truth

The Parental Deity and the One to Be Realized   25

God as the "Creator", God as "Good",   35
and God <u>As</u> the Real

The Culturally Prescribed "God"-Idea   49
of Exoteric Religion Is Not the Divine Itself
but Only a Cultural (and Entirely Conditional) Means
for Turning to the Divine

The Three Great Principles of All Truth   53

Real (Acausal) God Is The Deep of the World   57

True (or Real, or Esoteric) Religion Is Founded   67
on the <u>Direct</u> <u>Experiential</u> <u>Knowledge</u> of Reality

Glossary   77

An Invitation: Become a Formal Devotee   83
of Avatar Adi Da Samraj

The Avataric Divine Wisdom-Teaching of Adi Da Samraj   95

Introduction to
Religion and Reality

by Megan Anderson, Jonathan Condit, PhD, and Carolyn Lee, PhD

Adi Da Samraj once opened an essay with the provocative statement, "Religion is 'cult'". By definition, He went on to explain, religion is a "sacralized" system of philosophical and practical observances within the domain of time and space. Because it necessarily consists of defined beliefs and rituals, dependent on the existence of the concrete world in which it appears, Adi Da Samraj points out the self-evident fact that no religion can ever, in and of itself, be equal to Truth or Reality. Reality Itself is always senior to the cults of humankind.

So what is the right and true relationship between religion and Reality? *Religion and Reality* presents Avatar Adi Da's answer to that question.

Reality Itself Is the Only Real God

Real (Acausal) God is not a myth. Real (Acausal) God is not merely an idea. The Existence of Real (Acausal) God cannot be disproven. And, paradoxically, the Existence of Real (Acausal) God cannot even be proven. Rather, the Existence of Real (Acausal) God is Self-Evident, or Self-Affirming and Self-Authenticating—because Reality Itself Is Inherently The Case, Inherently True, and Inherently Divine.

—Avatar Adi Da Samraj

"Reality" (with a capital "R") is Avatar Adi Da's simplest reference to the Ultimate Condition that is the Prior Truth of existence. What appears in the world of beings is a myriad of always changing and passing forms and states. The Ultimate Condition is That Unbroken Reality Which neither arises nor passes away. Reality Itself is, as Avatar Adi Da has described, "Always Already the Case". Reality is in no way separate from anything that appears, because everything that appears is only an apparent modification of that Divine Reality Itself.

Of course, the Ultimate Reality is conceived by human beings in various ways. One of the principal descriptions of Ultimate Reality is as Great "Other" (often called "God"). But this conception, as Adi Da Samraj thoroughly addresses in the essays that follow, is based in childish and adolescent views. Presuming to be separate from a Prior Condition, human beings have looked to account for the appearance of all "things" and to feel "safe" in the face of their mortal condition.

However, while the concept of a "Creator/Parent God" is widespread, it is a myth. That Which truly could be called "God" (in the sense of the Ultimate Reality) does not cause the world to exist, nor cause any of the happenings in the world of appearances. The machine of the universe is its own cause, and is only caused from its own "point of view". Real God is the Divine Reality—the Acausal (or Non-causative) Condition within Which the universe arises.

In some ways, then, to most deeply receive Avatar Adi Da's Communication in this book is to be loosed from centuries of misunderstanding and to find the freedom to "consider" the real purpose of the world and the Nature of Real God as Reality Itself.

Exoteric and Esoteric Religion

True religion is not about the "me"-person who participates in religion. Rather, true religion is about the Divine—with Which any individual is re-associating, or re-uniting. True religion is, ultimately, about discovering Oneness with the Divine Self-Condition to be Always Already the Case.

—Avatar Adi Da Samraj

Side by side with His argument about Real (Acausal) God is Avatar Adi Da's clarification of the nature of true religion. True religion is a <u>process</u> (rather than a concretized "something")—one that involves constant surrender to Reality and that leads (ultimately) to the Realization of Reality Itself. Mere belief is not purposed to Realization, but only to consolation of the mortal self. The direct <u>experience</u> of Reality Itself is the true foundation of Reality-Realization. Religion on any other basis, Adi Da Samraj shows us, is a product of immaturity.

Adi Da Samraj distinguishes two categories of religious efforts that have developed in human history—the "exoteric" and the "esoteric". Popular, or <u>exoteric</u>, religion is motivated by the concerns of physical and social existence. Whatever its particular characteristics of doctrine and practice in any time and place, exoteric religion is a search for "salvation" through belief in some kind of "Creator-God" or patron-deity, and through adherence to a moral code of behavior that promotes social order.

The <u>esoteric</u> traditions, accounting for a small minority of humanity's religious endeavors, conduct a more refined and inward form of seeking. They aspire to transcend the common myths and Awaken directly to What is Ultimate. They all speak, in one manner or another, of Realizing an Ultimate Source-Condition of the impermanent, arising world. (Of course, this intention has various meanings and implications, depending on the orientation of the tradition.)

In the present age, the ancient esoteric (or "secret") traditions have become widely available outside the cultural milieu in which they developed. This is both a boon and a hazard. While the opportunity to grow beyond myth-based beliefs is offered now around the globe, we must also respect the profound preparatory practice that is the requirement of any true esoteric path.

The Three Elements of Conventional Religious Thinking

The "I"-thought (or the presumed-to-be-independent ego-self), and the world, and the "God"-idea are the three fundamental categories of Reality-as-reflection. As such, "ego-'I'", "world-out-there", and "God-everywhere" are the essential categories of egoic bondage—the tripartite package of world-mummery.

—Avatar Adi Da Samraj

Avatar Adi Da has given a beautifully simple summary of the core paradigm underlying all conventional religious thinking. This paradigm presumes that the basic "quantities" of existence are three in number—"self", "world", and "God". And this three-part paradigm accounts for the fundamental thought-structure (and also the basic modes of practice) of all religious and Spiritual traditions—both exoteric and esoteric.

Indeed, the presumed "split" between "self" and "other" (including both "world" and "God") is <u>the</u> "problem" to be resolved in all human philosophy and religion. That "split"— between "me" and "everything else" (including "God"), or between "inside" and "outside"—seems to be so obvious a feature of conditional existence that we usually do not question it at all. In fact, "belief" in that "split" is the cornerstone of our daily-life "philosophy"!

However, Avatar Adi Da has made a supremely "radical" Revelation about the nature of the "self"—which we presume to be, and which we presume is inherently "different" from "everything else". The separate "self" (or ego-"I") is, He says, not something we are being. Rather, the separate "self" (or ego-"I") is something we are doing. Or, as Adi Da has said countless times, "The ego is not an entity, but an activity."

The root-activity of the ego, Adi Da Reveals, is self-contraction. Presuming to be a separate (and, therefore, inherently threatened) "someone", every human being contracts (physically, emotionally, mentally, and with the breath) in the face of the apparent threat of everything "other". However, that activity of self-contraction is not inherent to the being. That activity of self-contraction is something each human being is doing in reaction to his or her (real or presumed) experience.

The Way of Adidam, which Avatar Adi Da has Revealed and Given, is the Way of the "radical" (or "at-the-root") transcending of the self-contraction. Only when such "radical" ego-transcendence is the case is it possible to truly "Know" Reality Itself. Thus, the "radical" transcending of egoity is an absolutely essential aspect of the Ultimate Reality-Realizing process Offered to all by Adi Da Samraj.

Grow Beyond Religion

Mere religion (or any and all religion in and of itself) must be transcended. . . . Religion must be established, in present-time, with reference to Reality Itself. Reality Itself Is Divine. Reality Itself Is all the God there Is. Only Reality Itself Is true religion.
—Avatar Adi Da Samraj

This book is itself preparation for Avatar Adi Da's further Revelations in the "Perfect Knowledge" Series as a whole. Only on the basis of outgrowing belief-based exoteric religion, and understanding the esoteric principle of true religion, are we prepared to receive the great Reality-Teachings that affirm the Ultimate Transcendental Truth, with no reference whatsoever to the world of arising forms and experience.

It is Avatar Adi Da's Impulse to Give all that is needed for the sake of right religious and Spiritual understanding in our time. His Teachings about religion and Reality are intended to unlock fundamental obstructions to our growth, such that we can ultimately awaken to Reality Itself. Avatar Adi Da's entire life is devoted to Revealing—and Being—the means for Reality Itself to Communicate directly in human time.

The Very One Who Is, Reality Itself, is by Nature moved to Liberate—to set beings free of identification with the web of illusions that makes up the usual life. This book is a gift from Adi Da Samraj to all who need to understand the human event from the viewpoint of Ultimate Truth, beyond the winds of doctrine and the competing philosophies that have made and unmade the cultures of humankind. ■

RELIGION AND REALITY

MOVING BEYOND
CHILDISH AND ADOLESCENT
APPROACHES
TO LIFE AND TRUTH

In the current exchanges about the True Way of life, people are alternately invited either to submit themselves in childish, emotional, and cultic fashion, usually by grace of "hype", to one or another glamorous tradition, personality, or possible effect, or else to assert their adolescent independence from any Divine Influence, Master, or Way by engaging in any one of the (seemingly numberless) cool, mental, and strategic methods of self-indulgence, self-absorption, self-help, de-programming, or certified sudden transcendentalism now available in these media-motivated times. In the midst of the pervasive language of these offerings is all the implicit crawling fear of children and adolescents, surrounded by Parent, waiting for Wednesday, wasting weekends on authorities who preach against authority, or who promote peculiar enthusiasms for secret, unique, scriptural, and wholly fulfilling techniques for bodily, emotional, and mental absorptions in the One True Reality—which everyone advertises, but very few find sufficient. Religious, Spiritual, and philosophical revivals are so plastic and popular, as mindless as soap—and, yet, they seem always to distract the world.

I am not the usual man. All that I Teach has been Awakened and Tested in My Own Case. There is Grace. There is Truth. There is Transcendental, Real, Acausal God, Which is both Reality and Truth. There are true and false (or fruitless) ways to live. There are partial revelations. What is only distraction and foolishness has always been part of the theatre of humankind. This need not be of concern, if the need for True Illumination is strong enough. What each one is obliged to do is to Realize, in his or her own case, a heart that is the center of one's life, that is neither self-indulgent nor foolish, and that is responsible only to Truth.

"Experiences", high and low, are required by those who are still lingering in the conditions of their childhood and adolescence. Everything a child does is a manifestation of one underlying presumption: dependence. When you are a child, the presumption of dependence is eminently realistic and useful. But it should be a temporary stage of psycho-physical life, in which one's functions are nurtured and developed in conventional ways. However, there is commonly a lag in the transition to adulthood, because of the shocks experienced in the immature attempts to function in the world. Thus, to some degree, every adult lingers in the childhood presumption of dependence. And, insofar as adults are children, they seek to enlarge that personal presumption of dependence into a universal conception in the form of the "God-Cosmos-Parent" game—the game of dependence upon (and obedience to) That upon Which all depends. That childish aspect in each individual always seeks to verify the condition of dependence in forms of safety and relative unconsciousness. That childish demand in every adult human being is the principal origin of exoteric religion. Exoteric religion is the search to be re-united, to experience the vital and emotional re-establishment of some imagined or felt condition or state of life that is previous to responsibility. It is the urge toward the parented, enclosed condition. This urge always seeks experiences, beliefs, and immunities as a consolation for the primitive cognition of fear and vulnerability. And the "Way" enacted by such a motivation is principally a game of obedience to parent-like enormities.

It is in childhood that the idea of "God-Apart", or "Reality-Beyond", is conceived. The sense of dependence initiates the growing sense of separate and separated self through the experiential theatre of growth. The intuition of the Whole, the One, is the ground of birth—but "growing up" is a conventional pattern of initiation in which the sense of "difference" is intensified. At the conventional level of the life-functions themselves, there is a need for such functional practical differentiation—but the implications in the plane of consciousness are the cause of an unnatural adventure of suffering and seeking-in-dilemma.

The passage of childhood thus becomes the ground for the eventual conception of the mutually exclusive trinity of "God-Apart", separate self, and world-in-itself (any world, high or low). The drama implied in the added presumptions of independent self and objective world is generated at a later phase of life than childhood. The child barely comprehends the full force of implication inherent in the concepts of "ego" and "world of things". The child's principal concern is relative to the "God-Parent-Reality" (or That on Which all depends), and relative to his or her growing (but, as yet, not fully conscious) sense of separated self-existence. "Separate self" and "objective world" are yet hidden in unconsciousness for the child. They are (themselves) a mysterious and later comprehension of that which is (at first) only felt, not conceptualized, as fear and sorrow. Therefore, the child is always grasping for permanent security in an undifferentiated, unborn bliss, wherein the threats implied in life are forgotten and unknown. Re-union through obedience is the way the living child learns in secret, while the life that grows the child through experience continually demonstrates the failure of all childish seeking.

There must be a transition from childhood to maturity. That transition is commonly acknowledged as a stage in the psycho-physical development of the human being. It is called "adolescence". Like childhood, this stage also tends to be prolonged indefinitely—and, indeed, perhaps the majority of "civilized" human beings are occupied with the concerns of this transition most of their lives. The transitional stage of adolescence is marked by a sense of dilemma, just as the primal stage of childhood is marked by a sense of dependence. It is in this transitional stage that the quality of living one's existence as a dilemma is conceived. It is the dilemma imposed by the conventional presumption of separate, egoic, independent consciousness—and, thus, separative habits and action. That presumption is (altogether) the inevitable inheritance from childhood—and its clear, personal comprehension, felt over against the childish urge to dependence, is what initiates the ambivalent conflicts of the phase of adolescence.

The dilemma of adolescence is a continual goad to dramatization. It is the drama of the double-bind of dependence versus independence. Adolescence is the origin of cleverness and, in general, of mind. What we conventionally call the "conscious mind" is a strategic version of mind which is always manufacturing motivations. And, in the adolescent, these motivations (or desires) are mutually exclusive (or contradictory). This is because the adolescent is always playing with impulsive allegiance to two mutually exclusive principles: dependence and independence. The early (or childhood) condition yields the tendency to presume dependence—but the conventional learning of childhood, as well as the inherent growth-pattern of the individual psycho-physical being, yields (to the growing person) the equally powerful tendency to presume independence. The result is conventional consciousness (or "conscious mind"), as opposed to the unconsciousness of childhood—but that conventional consciousness is strategic in nature, and its foundation is the conception of life-as-dilemma. Therefore, adolescence is the origin of the great search in all adult human beings. Adolescence is an eternally failed condition, an irrevocable double-bind. It is the very form of "Narcissus"—the eternal self-absorption (or immunity) achieved by impulsive psycho-physical flight from the impositions of relational life.

The solutions developed in the adolescent theatre of human life phase between the exotic and exclusive extremes of either yielding to the state of egoic dependence (thus tending to disintegrate character) or asserting the status of egoic independence (thus tending to rigidify character). Both extremes remain tenuous, threatened by the possibility of the opposite destiny, and involve an ongoing sense of dilemma. Humanity makes "culture" and adventure out of such ambivalence. In the case of the yielding toward the childish condition of dependence, there is more of the mystical-invocatory-absorbed tendency. In the case of the revolutionary assertion of independence, there is more of the analytical-materialistic-discriminative tendency. In the adolescent range between these two extremes are all of the traditional and usual solutions of humankind, including the common understanding of religious and Spiritual life.

Traditional Spirituality, in the forms in which it is most commonly proposed or presumed, is a characteristically adolescent creation that represents an attempted balance between the extremes. It is not a life of <u>mere</u> (or simple) absorption in the mysterious enclosure of existence. It is a life of <u>strategic</u> absorption. It raises the relatively non-strategic and unconscious life of childhood dependence to the level of a fully strategic conscious life of achieved dependence (or absorption). Its goal is not merely psychological re-union, but total psychic release into some (imagined or felt) "Home" of being.

By the time the child fully achieves the life-strategy of obedience to That on Which all depends, he or she has entered the phase of adolescence. At that point, the individual fully presumes the ego-self and the world as apparently independent (or objective) dimensions, exclusive of (or other than) the "Reality" that is the goal of all dependence. Therefore, the path of obedience, fully developed, is already a path of dilemma, of conflict, of struggle with self—as every religious person comes to know by experience. Truly, then, the experiential fruition of the life-strategy of childhood (or dependence) is fully demonstrated only in the advent of human adolescence.

In every form of its adventure, the path of experience-and-attainment conceived in adolescence is a struggle for solutions to a principal dilemma. And that dilemma is (itself) the characteristic quality of all such adventures, as well as of the ordinary suffering of the usual human being. In adolescence, the separate, separated, and separative self is the motivating presumption behind the common suffering and the common heroism of humanity—both in life and in Spirit. The sense of permanently independent existence is the source of the dilemma that undermines the undifferentiated dependence of mere birth. In the adolescent, there is the unrelenting search for the success, self-fulfillment, unthreatened security, immunity, healing, extreme longevity, immortality, and ultimate salvation of the presumed ego-"I". The ego, "self", or "soul" is the primary presumption of the adolescent—just as "God-Apart", or That on Which all depends, is the primary presumption of the child. Therefore, in the usual human being, who is embedded in the adolescent conception of existence, the idea of "God" becomes in doubt, or is chronically resisted. Thus, "sin" (or "missing the mark") enters into the mind of adolescence. And the world becomes merely a scene of the adolescent drama in which even the very "stuff" of the world is viewed as a problem, a principal warfare of opposites, and in which the manipulation of conditionally manifested things (rather than Realization of the Eternally Present Nature, Condition, Form, and Process of Reality Itself) becomes the hope of peace.

There is a mature, real, and true phase of human life. Real and true human maturity is free of all childish things and free of all that is attained, acquired, and made in the adolescent adventures of conventional life. In that mature phase, the principle of separation is undermined by means of Real self-understanding, and the mutually exclusive trinity of "God", self, and world is returned to the Condition of Truth. In the maturity of human life, the world is not abandoned, nor is it lived as the scene of adolescent theatre, the adventure in dilemma. "God-Apart" occupies the child, and separate self occupies the adolescent—and both child and adolescent see the world only in terms of their own distinct limiting principle (or characteristic form of suffering). But, in the mature human being, the <u>world</u>—or the totality of all arising (subjective and objective, high and low), not as an exclusive "reality" but in Truth—is primary. In the mature individual, the world is (potentially) apprehended as a modification of the Single, Absolute, Non-separate Reality—implying no separate "self" or outside "God". For such a one, the Absolute Reality and the world are not "different". The Absolute Reality is the Divine Nature, Condition, Form, and Process of all-and-All. It Includes all that is manifest, and all that is unmanifest—all universes, conditions, beings, states, and things, all that is "within" and all that is "without", all that is visible and all that is invisible, all that is "here" and all that is "there", all dimensions of space-time and All that is Prior to space-time.

Clearly, the search for fulfillment via experiences of all kinds is the principal characteristic of both the childish and the adolescent stages of human development. The experiential dimension of the Divine Transforming Power contains every possibility for the holy or unholy fascination of children and adolescents. Therefore, I must always Work to Disentangle human beings from their lingering strategic life-motives—so that they may enter into the final (or mature) phase of life. It is only on the basis of such human maturity that life in Truth may be Realized and the experiential drama of unconsciousness, egoity, conventional mind, and strategic motivation may be understood.

The mature phase of human life is not characterized by either unconscious dependence or the strategically conscious dilemma of dependence-independence. It is the phase of feeling-attention (rather than dependence) and real human responsibility (rather than exclusive independence). As in childhood, there is no "problem"-based strategy at the root of the mature phase of life. Childhood is a realm of unconsciousness, whereas the mature person is freely conscious. Unlike the adolescent, the mature human being conceives no irreducible dilemma in life and conscious awareness.

This mature phase of life requires, as its ongoing foundation, the (at least eventual) most fundamental understanding of the egoic self. The separate and separative principle of independent self, the strategies of mind and desires, the usual ego-possessed life of the avoidance of relationship, the urges toward unconscious dependence and mechanical or wild independence, and all the mediocre solutions that temporarily balance or fulfill the extremes of experience— all of these must be obviated in most fundamental self-understanding. The mature (or responsible and truly conscious) phase of life is, thus, the origin of the real practice of life (or true action). And the mature phase of life, fully demonstrated, is characterized not by the usual religious and Spiritual "solutions", but by no-seeking, no-dilemma, no orientation toward the goal of any conceived or remembered state or condition. Only in the mature phase of life can you grow to Realize the Perfectly Prior (and, thus, always Present) Nature and Condition That Is Reality. Only a human being thus free enjoys conditionally manifested existence in (and as) the Very Nature and Condition and Heart of the Real (and Perfectly Acausal) Divine, Which is also the Process and Form and Light and Fullness of the worlds.

THE PARENTAL DEITY
AND THE ONE TO BE REALIZED

There is a common notion people have which they associate with "God" (or the Divine), and which they commonly identify as a basic religious feeling or concept. It may be described as a feeling that, even when you are alone, there is "Somebody Else" in the room. This is just the opposite (or the antithesis) of the "Point of View" of Real Spiritual life. I Speak about "God" all the time—but I am Speaking from a "Point of View" that is entirely different from the conventional religious one. Perhaps, by contrast, you could say that this "Point of View" is summarized in the notion that, no matter how many people are in the room, there is still only One Person there!

In general, discussions about "God" or religion tend to be naively associated with the idea of the Power that is "Other", or the One Who is "Other". This "God"-idea corresponds to a rather childish (or even infantile) sense of Reality. Children are not, in general, great metaphysicians or great mystics! They have some very primitive kinds of awareness, as well as some remarkable kinds of awareness that adults tend to lose or dismiss. However, when children communicate their sense of "God", they very often express a feeling that has been dictated to them by their parents. They naively describe Reality according to a child's psychology—that child-made awareness of Reality which is not natively associated with great, abstract propositions. It is not that children are free of mind, and (therefore) their religious concepts are purer than those of adults. The religious concepts to which a child can be sensitive and responsive are generally built upon the psychology of the childhood situation—which is one of being dependent on a parent or parents, particularly on the mother. The parent-child relationship—in which the parent is a great, experienced person there to protect the smaller, vulnerable person—provides the naive basis for childish religious views and for what is commonly called "religious" views in general. In other words, the notion that people have of "God"—apart from Real-God-Realization Itself—tends to be a carryover, an extension of your childish situation. Therefore, religion tends to be a solution for a rather infantile problem: the need to be protected, sustained, and made to feel that everything is all right and that everything is going to be all right, the need to feel that there is a superior "Other" that is in charge of everything.

When people communicate to their children about "God", they commonly speak of "God" as a kind of super-version of mommy-and-daddy. When people speak to one another about their earliest religious consciousness (and it is more a kind of conventionally acquired mental attitude than it is an experience), they commonly talk to one another in terms of a child's model of Reality. However, to truly enter into the religious process, you must transcend the child's version of Reality. To become human, to be an adult, a mature human personality, you should have overcome that childish view—but, commonly, people do not. Thus, to the degree that people are religious (in the conventional manner), it is that portion of themselves that is basically childish or infantile that is being religious or that needs religion.

The entire domain of conventional religion is (commonly) the domain of immaturity—or of childishness and adolescence, rather than real human maturity. When people believe in "God", what they are actually believing is that everything that is outside of themselves is ultimately epitomized in some Person, Force, or Being that is not merely making and controlling everything, but is in charge and is going to protect them—and, especially, that this "Other" Person will protect them and even help them to get a lot of things they want, if they will enter into a special kind of relationship with that One. That relationship is very similar to the one that you were called to enter into with your parents: "Be good—and we will love you, and protect you, and give you things that you want."

Thus, popular (or conventional) religion is largely a cultural domain of social morality. People are asked to behave in one or another fashion that one would call "good" in order to maintain a good association with the parent-like "God", so that they will be loved and protected by that One and given the things they want (while they are alive, and after death).

Conventional religion is largely an enterprise of childhood—of the dependent, childish state. When people become adults, however, they have more hard facts to deal with in life. They feel much less protected than they did as children in the household of their parents. So they begin to question and to doubt the existence of this Parental Deity. Such individuals may continue to be conventionally religious in some sense, willing to play the game of social morality and good behavior—but they carry on a rather adolescent relationship of dependence-independence, or embrace and withdrawal, relative to this "God-Person".

Atheism is the ultimate form of denial of the Parental "God". Atheism is not founded on real experience of the ultimate facts of the universe. Rather, it is a kind of adolescent development of the human species. What characterizes the doctrine (or dogma) of atheism is not a discovery that there is no "God", but a refusal to acknowledge every kind of parent (or parent-like authority), including (therefore) the Parental "God" of childish religion.

If conventional religion amounts to an actual experience (rather than just a kind of conventionally acquired state of mind), it could basically be defined as a very primitive sense that invades all of your life, but that relates to you most specifically in your solitariness, your private individuality. It is the sense that, when you are alone—and you are, in the sense that you have a private destiny, always alone—there is always "Somebody Else", the "Great Parent", always there. That One, it is presumed, sees everything you do, and represents a "Parental Will" relative to what you do. That One wants you to do certain things, wants you not to do other things, and will presumably reward you if you do the things that It wants you to do and will punish you in various ways if you do not do those things. Out of this kind of "Parent-God"-ism come all the other traditions associated with the notions of "sin", or the valuation of events not merely factually but in terms of the Parental Deity. In other words, if something negative happens to you, it is generally regarded as a Divinely given punishment or a result of what you have done in terms of your social personality and your conventional moral activity. If good things happen to you, they are presumed to be gifts or rewards from the same Source.

Examine the "point of view" of conventional "downtown" (or popular) religion. You will see that it corresponds to this structure of notions, and is (therefore) primarily a development of a child's state of awareness. It is a development of the original parent-bond of your childhood, and it is complicated by the dissociative individuation that develops in adolescence, and that tends to characterize your adulthood as well.

The only-by-Me Revealed and Given Way of Adidam is not a form of this childish (or conventional) religion. When I Speak of Real (Acausal) God (and I also use other terms than "Real Acausal God", but that is one of the forms of reference I use), I am not speaking of a Parental Deity. I have frequently had occasion to Criticize this childish mode of relating to "God" and to the entire process of religion and Spiritual life. I could compare the true "Point of View" that I "Consider" with you to the conventional or childish religious "point of view" by saying that true religion is not founded in the primitive feeling that, even when you are alone, there is always "Someone Else" present. Rather, I Describe the basis of true religion as a mysterious experience or intuition that—no matter how many others are present, no matter how many people are present, including yourself, no matter what is arising—there is only One Reality, One Self-Condition, One Source-Condition. That One is not "Other". That One is not your parent. And, in phenomenal and experiential terms, That One is not merely devoted to rewarding and punishing you, supporting you and protecting you. Rather, That One is the Acausal Divine Self-Condition (and Source-Condition) of all phenomenal conditions—including all opposites, even all contradictions. Thus, you cannot account for That One in childish terms.

In fact, if you really examine the characteristics of conditional Nature (or of phenomenal existence), there is no justification for believing in the Parental Deity at all. It is simply not true to the facts of existence altogether that there is a Great Omniscient, Omnipresent, Omnipotent Being making everything happen—in charge of everything happening, and making things turn out well for those who acknowledge That One and obey certain moral principles. It is simply not so. It is not true that there is such a Parental Deity controlling history, controlling even all events, and working out a great "success-plan" for humanity.

The Acausal Divine, or Real (Acausal) God, the One to be Realized, is not other than Reality Itself. That One Transcends your personal, conditional existence—but your conditional existence arises in That One. All of this conditionally arising world is a modification of That One, a "play" upon That One. To Realize That One, you must enter profoundly into the Inherently egoless Self-Position—but not by means of the traditional method of inversion, or turning attention inward. That inward-turning effort is simply one of the ego-based solutions to the presumed problem of existence. That Which must be Realized is in the Perfectly Subjective Self-Position—and It is Realized not by appeal to Something outside yourself nor by entering into childish dependence in relation to some great Principle, but by transcending your own separative (and self-contracting) activity, and (thereby, ultimately, by Means of My Avataric Divine Spiritual Grace) Realizing Most Perfect Identification with That in Which you Always Already Inhere.

All of the public religious chitchat, the seemingly endless worldly conversation, about whether "God" exists or not, is simply a continuation of the doubting and subjective mulling-over of problem-consciousness that is part of the adolescence of humankind. Always wondering about whether "God" exists is simply an adult occupation of basically adolescent personalities whose notions of "God" were formed by the childhood situation of dependence. Thus, wondering about whether "God" exists is basically an effort to prove the existence of the "God" you believed in as a child. Nevertheless, the "God" you believed in as a child does <u>not</u> exist—not as It was then described to you, nor as you then believed. What you are told (in childhood) about "God" is communicated in terms that your parents hope will satisfy your needs as a child. In other words, parents develop your "God-consciousness" (or your religious orientation) when you are a child as an extension of what they themselves are otherwise trying to do as parents. Parents naturally want their children to feel protected. They do not want their children to become neurotic and to feel threatened. And they want their children to learn how to behave as expected. They want their children to develop socializing tendencies, to learn how to relate to others positively and to function socially, how to survive socially and in ordinary human terms. This is what parents want you to do—and, in some ordinary sense, it is natural enough for them to want you to do this. Thus, when parents teach religion to their children, they teach them (as a general rule) about a "God" who is basically a poetic extension of themselves as parents.

Parents do not want their children to feel unprotected—but, really, the source of children's protection is their parents,

31

and the community, and the human world altogether. Apart from whatever protection people can generate for children as their parents and as the community that surrounds them, children really are not very well protected. And neither is anyone else! Beyond what you can do for one another as human beings cooperating with each other, there is very little protection in this world for anyone. So you do want your children to feel protected, but <u>you</u> are protecting them. There is no reason to invent a Santa Claus "Parent-God" to make them feel protected. You should let your children know that you are protecting them, that you are providing them with circumstances in which they will be able to live and not be threatened, and in which they are loved quite naturally by others.

Really, children should understand that becoming a positive social personality is not supposed to be a way of getting the goods from "God" or getting love from "the Parent". In that syndrome, love is different from your own social activity, and your social activity is a way of getting love. What you should be teaching your children is that to become a relational personality means that you <u>become</u> love. <u>You</u> must become love. Human beings must become loving. Thus, social activities are not supposed to be something you do in order to get love. Your interpersonal activities should <u>be</u> love. The whole notion of "sin" as a result of violating the "Ultimate Parent" is not something you should communicate to your children.

As My devotee, you do not become truly religious unless you truly understand My Avataric Divine Wisdom-Teaching and Awaken to Its "Point of View". The Parental "God" of childish religion cannot be proven to exist—because that One does <u>not</u> exist. The struggle to prove the existence of such a One is a false struggle. It is an expression of the common disease, the problem-consciousness of threatened egoity. This does not mean that you should become like scientific materialists, and, atheistically, throw religion away. Much of what is conventionally called "religion" <u>should</u> be thrown away, based on a very intelligent "consideration"—because it is just a form of man-made consolation for rather childish egos. However, there is much more to true religion than what is contained in these childish propositions. It is What <u>Is</u>, Beyond these childish propositions, that I Call you to "consider" in the form of My Own Teaching-Argument, and also in the evidence of the Great Tradition of humankind (or the total global inheritance of human culture).

There <u>Is</u> the Great Being, the Great Divine Reality. There Is That Truth. And there is a Way of entering into the Realization of That One. It requires great maturity—not child-ishness, not adolescence, not egoity—and It involves the transcending of everything conventionally religious that is associated with your childish and adolescent personality. You enter into that Realization not by appealing to the Power of the "Other", the presumed objective Parental Deity outside you, as proposed by conventional religion. The only-by-Me Revealed and Given Way of Adidam does not involve appeal to that Great "Other" One—not even an appeal to that "Other" One in the form of mystical (or subtle) objects of any kind. The God who truly and Really Exists is not the white-bearded Character of popular religious mythology. The God who truly and Really Exists is not even some kind of all-pervading Parent-like Essence. The God Who truly and Really Exists is not present as a separate (or exclusively "Other") Personality <u>anywhere</u> in cosmic Nature. Nor is That One to be identified with any subtle object in Nature, or with any of the lights observable via mystical consciousness. That One <u>Is</u> Real (Acausal) God. You Realize—and, thereby (ultimately), prove the Existence of—That One only by entering most profoundly into the Inherently egoless Self-Domain (or Self-Position), the Domain of Prior Existence (or <u>Is</u>-ness), the Tacit Self-Apprehension of Being (Itself).

The "God" of cosmic Nature, the "Creator-God", cannot be proven—because that One does not exist as proposed. Real (Acausal) God Is the Transcendental, Inherently Spiritual, Inherently egoless, and Self-Evidently Divine Person—Self-Existing and Self-Radiant. Real (Acausal) God Exists at the level of Eternal Existence and not at the level of the objects related to your conditional egoic existence (or your conditionally manifested independence). Real (Acausal) God is the One in Whom all others, all objects, and all states of cosmic Nature Inhere. Only That One is Avatarically Incarnate as the Divine Heart-Master, the One Who Reveals and Gives the Most Perfect Realization of the Divine Self-Condition.

I Am The Divine Heart-Master—Self-Revealed and Self-Given As and by Means of Spiritual Force, Transmitted by the Graceful Means of My Avataric Divine Spirit-Baptism. The Purpose of My Spirit-Baptism is not to call you to conform to an apparent Power of "Otherness" outside yourself, which requires you to engage in activities similar to the childish social routines of conventional religiosity. Rather, the Purpose of My Spirit-Baptism is to Awaken you to the Realization of That Which is in the Inherently egoless Self-Position.

Thus, the Truth That is to be Realized may be summarized simply as the Realization that no matter what is arising, no matter how many others are present, there Is Only One Being. This is precisely different from the childish proposition that even when you are alone there is always "Someone Else" present.

GOD AS THE "CREATOR", GOD AS "GOOD", AND GOD AS THE REAL

Conventional "God"-religion originates in the state of mind that characterizes the first three stages of life. Thus, conventional "God"-religion is ego-based—and it serves the functional desire of the egoic (or phenomenal) self to be protected, nourished, pleasurized, and (ultimately) preserved.

The phenomenal self, or egoic (self-centered) body-mind, is the source of conventional "God"-religion, as well as all of the other ordinary and extraordinary pursuits of born existence in the first six stages of life. Therefore, it is not <u>Real</u> God but the ego (perhaps gesturing conceptually toward "God") that is the source and fundamental subject of popular (or exoteric) religion (as well as higher mysticism). Real Spiritual life begins only when the ego (with all of its mind, emotion, desire, and activity) is thoroughly understood and (thereby) transcended. For this reason, only the only-by-Me Revealed and Given "Radical" (and Perfectly Counter-egoic) Wisdom-Teaching of the seventh stage of life <u>directly</u> Serves the process of Most Perfect Real-God-Realization. All other forms of doctrine (or instruction) serve the purposes of the first six stages of life—all of which are founded on the egoic presumption of "self-and-other".

It is the culture of conventional religion that promotes conventional ideas about "God". The principal conventional "God"-idea is that "God" is the "Creator" (or intentional Emanator) of the worlds and all beings. Such seems an obvious idea to the bodily ego, trapped in the mechanics of the perceptual mind and the material (or elemental) vision. The ego is identified with embodiment, and the idea of the "Creator-God" is developed to account for this fact, and to provide a conceptual basis (in the form of the idea of the ego as "God-made creature") for the appeal to "God" to Help the ego in this world and in the (yet unknown) after-death state.

The difficulty with the "Creator-God" conception is that it identifies "God" with ultimate causation and (thus) makes

"God" inherently responsible for the subsequent causation of all effects. And, if "God" is responsible for all effects, then "God" is clearly a very powerful but also terrible Deity—since conditionally manifested existence tends to work both for and against all "creatures".

Therefore, in conventional religious thinking, the "Creator-God"-idea is commonly coupled with the idea of "God" as "Good" (and, thus, both opposite and opposed to "Evil"). If the "Creator-God" is conceived to be "Good" (or always working to positively "create", protect, nourish, rightly and pleasurably fulfill, and, ultimately, preserve all of conditional Nature and all "creatures"—insofar as they are rightly aligned to "God"), then the ego is free of the emotional double-bind and the anger and despair that would seem to be justified if "God" is simply the responsible "Creator" of everything (good, bad, or in-between). Therefore, conventional religious theology is founded on both the idea of "God" as "Creator" <u>and</u> the idea of "God" as "Good" (or "Good Will").

However, if God is the All-Powerful "Creator" (except for Whose activities not anything has been made), then how did so much obviously negative (or evil) motion and effect come into existence? The usual answer is generally organized around one or another mythological story in which powerful creatures (or one powerful creature, such as "Satan", regarded to personify "Evil") entered (on the basis of free will) into a pattern of "sin" (or disobedience and conflict in relation to "God")—which resulted in separation from "God", and a descent (or fall) into gross (material) bondage, and so forth. Such mythologies are structured in terms of a hierarchical view of conditional Nature, with various planes descending from the "Heaven" of "God". Religion (thus) becomes a method of "return" to "God".

Exoteric religion (or the "God"-religion of the first three stages of life) is generally based on an appeal to belief, social morality, and magically effective prayer or worship. The "return" to "God" is basically conceived in terms of this world—and, therefore, exoteric (or terrestrial) religion is actually a process in which "God" returns to the ego and to this world (rather than vice versa), and it is believed that "God" will eventually reclaim humankind and the total world from the forces of "Evil". Nevertheless, exoteric religion is an "outer cult", intended for grosser egos and for mass consumption (or the culture of the first three stages of life). The most advanced form of conventional "God"-religion is the esoteric (or inner) "cult"—which is a mystical society, open only to those chosen for initiation (and, thus, growth, or development, into the fourth and fifth stages of life). Esoteric "God"-religion is a process of cosmic mysticism, or the method of "return" to "God" by ascending as mind (or disembodied "soul")—back through the route of the original fall into matter and "Evil"—until the "Heaven" (or "Eternal Abode") of "God" is reached again. This esoteric mystical process goes beyond the conventions of exoteric religion to develop the psycho-physical mechanics of mystical flight and "return" to "God" via the hierarchical structures of the nervous system (ascending from the plane of "Evil", or "Satan", or the "flesh", at the bodily base of the nervous system, to the plane of "God", or the plane of "Good", or the "Heavenly Abode", at or above the brain, via the "magic carpet" of the life-force in the nervous system).

Thus, the idea of the "Creator-God" leads to the idea that "God" is "Good" (or "Good Will"), which leads to the idea that "creatures" have free will, which then accounts for the appearance of "sin", suffering, "Evil", and loss of "God-consciousness". And conventional "God"-religion then becomes the means (through structures of belief, sacramental worship, mystical prayer, Yogic or shamanistic ascent, and so forth) for the re-exercise of "creaturely" free will in the direction of "God", "Good", the triumph over "Evil" and death in this world, and the ascent from material form and consciousness to Spiritual, "Heavenly", or "Godly" form and consciousness.

All the popular and mystical religious and Spiritual traditions of humankind tend to be associated with this chain of conceptions (or the characteristic ideas of the first five stages of life). It is only in the sixth stage traditions that these ideas begin to give way to different conceptions. It is only in the sixth stage of life that the egoic basis of the first five stages of life is penetrated. And it is only in the only-by-Me Revealed and Given seventh stage of life that the ego is most perfectly transcended in the Divine Reality (Itself).

The theological and general religious conceptions I have just Described have always been subject to criticism (or at least simple non-belief) on the part of those who are not persuaded by religious and theological arguments. Atheism (or the conception that no "Creator-God"—or any other Greater Reality—exists) has always opposed theism (or "God"-religion). Nevertheless, atheistic ideas are the product of the same fundamental egoic consciousness that otherwise produces theistic (or conventional religious) ideas. Atheism is the product of the ego (or the phenomenal self, grounded in elemental perception), and so also is theism. Atheism, like exoteric "God"-religion, extends itself only into the domain of the first three stages of life—whereas <u>esoteric</u> "God"-religion provides a means for entering, mystically and Spiritually, into the developmental processes of the fourth stage of life and the fifth stage of life.

Atheism regularly proposes a "logic" of life that has its own dogmatic features. It does not propose a "God"-idea but, instead, founds itself on and in the perceptual and phenomenal mind alone. Atheism concedes only a universal and ultimately indifferent (or merely lawful) <u>Nature</u> (not a "God")—and, so, there is no need to create a religious "creation myth" to account for suffering. (And atheistic thinkers thus generally confine themselves to constructing a cosmology, based on material observations alone, that merely accounts for the apparent workings of the conditionally manifested events of cosmic Nature.) Indeed, just as conventional "God"-religion (or conventional theism) arises to account for suffering, atheism arises on the basis of the unreserved acknowledgment of suffering. And, if there is no idea of "God", there is no idea of the human being as "creature" (or, in other words, the human being as the bearer of an immortal, or "God-like", inner part). Nor is there any need to interpret unfortunate or painful events as the effects of "Evil". Therefore, the atheistic "point of view" is characterized by the trend of mind called "realism", just as the conventional religious (or theistic) "point of view" is characterized by the trend of mind called "idealism"—but both atheism and theism arise on the basis of the self-contraction (or the ego of phenomenal self-consciousness), rather than on the basis of direct Intuition of the Real Condition That is Prior to separate self and its conventions of perception and thought.

The realistic (or atheistic) view is just as much the bearer of a myth (or a merely conceptual interpretation of the world) as is the conventional religious (or theistic) view. Atheism (or conventional realism) is a state of mind which is based in the phenomenal self and which seeks the ultimate protection, nourishment, pleasure, and preservation of the phenomenal self (at least in this world and, if there should be an after-life, then also in any other world). Therefore, atheism (or conventional realism) is simply a philosophical alternative to theism (or conventional "God"-religion), based on the same principle and consciousness (which is the phenomenal ego), and seeking (by alternative means) to fulfill the conditionally manifested self and relieve it of its suffering.

Atheism (or conventional realism) is a state of mind that possesses individuals who are fixed in the first three stages of life. It is a form of "spiritual neurosis" (or ego-possession), as are all of the characteristic mind-states of the first six stages of life. Esoteric "God"-religion provides a basis for certain remarkable individuals to enter the fourth stage of life and the fifth stage of life, but the commonly (or exoterically) religious individual is, like the atheist, a relatively adolescent (if not childish, and even infantile) character, fixed in the ego-possessed states characteristic of the first three stages of life.

Atheism proposes a myth and a method for ego-fulfillment that is based on phenomenal realism, rather than religious idealism (or the culture of the conventional "God"-idea). Therefore, atheism is traditionally associated with the philosophy of materialism—just as theism is associated with "Creationism", and "Emanationism", and conventional (or mystical—or fourth and fifth stage) Spirituality. And the realistic (or atheistic) view tends to be the foundation for all kinds of political, social, and technological movements, since its orientation is toward the investigation and manipulation of material Nature.

Atheism is realism and materialism. It is about the acquisition of knowledge about conditional Nature and the exploitation of that knowledge to command (or gain power over) conditional Nature. And it is this scheme of knowledge and power (expressed as political and technological means of all kinds) that is the basis of the mythology and quasi-religion of atheism. The atheistic (or non-theistic) view of life is ego-based, organized relative to conditional Nature as an elemental (or grossly perceived) process, and committed to knowledge and power as the means of "salvation" (or material fulfillment of egoity).

In this "late-time" (or "dark" epoch), the materialistic, realistic, and non-theistic philosophy of ego-fulfillment is represented by the world-culture of scientific, technological, and political materialism. The entire race of humankind is now being organized by the cultural movement of scientific materialism—which counters (and even seeks to suppress) the alternative cultures of exoteric religion, esoteric mysticism, Transcendental Self-Realization, and Divine Enlightenment. Scientism (or the culture of realistic or materialistic knowledge) and its two arms of power (technology and political order) are the primary forces in world-culture at the present time. And humanity at large is (thus) tending to be reduced to the robotic acculturations of orderly egoism in the limited terms represented by humanity's functional development in the first three stages of life.

Conventional and popular human culture has historically been limited to the conflicts and alternatives represented by theism and atheism, or egoic idealism and egoic realism. And the large-scale ordering of humankind has always tended to be dominated by the politics of materialistic knowledge and power. It is simply that in the "late-time" (or "dark" epoch), the materialistic culture is approaching the status of a worldwide mass-culture in which all individuals will be controlled by a powerful and materialistically oriented system of political and technological restriction.

The usual (or most commonly remarked) criticism of theism (or conventional "God"-religion) is based on the evidence of suffering and material limitation. Therefore, the common arguments against theism are generally those proposed by the "point of view" of atheism. Likewise, the common arguments against atheism are generally those proposed by theism (which are based on an egoic appeal to the evidence of religious history, cultic revelation, mystical psychology, and psychic experience). For this reason, there may seem to be only two basic cultural alternatives: atheism and theism.

Theism and conventional "God"-religion are, at base, an expression of egoity in the first three stages of life—just as is the case with atheism and conventional materialism. Therefore, whenever theism (or conventional "God"-religion) becomes the base for political and social order, it inevitably becomes the base for knowledge and power in the material world. And exoterically theistic regimes have historically been equally as aggressive in the manipulation and suppression of humanity as have atheistic regimes. Exoteric theism is, at its base, egoic and fitted to worldly concerns. Therefore, when it achieves worldly power, it simply adopts the same general materialistic means that are adopted by atheism. Knowledge and power are the common tools of egoity, not merely the tools of atheism. In its esoteric forms, theism (or conventional "God"-religion) can, via the exercises and attainments of Saints and mystics, apply knowledge and power to purposes that extend beyond the first three stages of life. However, in the terms of the first three stages of life (or the common and practical social order), theism (or conventional "God"-religion) is inclined to make the same demands for social consciousness—and to apply fundamentally the same kind of political and authoritarian techniques for achieving obedience and order—as atheism and scientism.

And the more important esoteric matters of Spiritual Wisdom, mystical knowledge, and the magical power of Sainthood or Adeptship are as much in doubt and disrepute in the common religious circles of theism as they are in scientific and atheistic circles.

All of this is to indicate that conventional "God"-religion (or theism)—and even all religious and Spiritual pursuits of the first six stages of life—share a root-error (or limitation) with atheism and worldly culture. That error (or limitation) is the ego itself, or the presumptions and the seeking that are most basic to the conception of an independent phenomenal self in a (less than hospitable) phenomenal world. Thus, what is ultimately to be criticized in conventional "God"-religion (or theism) is the same limit that is to be criticized in atheism and materialism. It is the ego, the phenomenal self-base—from which people tend to derive their conceptions of "God", Nature, life, and destiny.

It is only when the egoic root of one's functional, worldly, and religious or Spiritual life is inspected, understood, and transcended that self, and world, and God are seen in Truth. Therefore, it is necessary to understand your own egoic activity. It is necessary to aspire to Wisdom, Truth, and Enlightenment. All occupations derived from the ego-base are (necessarily) limited to egoity, and all conceptions that feed such egoic occupations are (necessarily) bereft of a right view of self, world, and Real God (Which Is the Acausal Divine Reality and Truth).

When the mechanics of egoity are transcended in self-understanding, then it becomes obvious that life (or conditionally manifested phenomenal existence) is simply a "play" of opposites. Neither "Good" (or "creation" and preservation) nor "Evil" (or destruction) finally wins. Conditional Nature, in all its planes, is inherently a dynamic. The "play" of conditional Nature, in all its forms and beings and processes, is not merely (or exclusively and finally) seeking the apparent "Good" of self-preservation (or the preservation and fulfillment of any particular form, world, or being), nor is it merely (or exclusively and finally) seeking the apparent "Evil" of self-destruction (or the dissolution of any particular form, world, or being). Rather, the "play" in conditional Nature is always in the direction of perpetuating the dynamics of the "play" itself—and, therefore, polarity, opposition, struggle, alternation, death, and cyclic repetition tend to be perpetuated as the characteristics of phenomenal existence. Therefore, the "play" of Nature is always alternating between the appearance of dominance by one or the other of its two basic extremes. And the sign of this is in the inherent struggle that involves every conditionally apparent form, being, and process. The struggle is this dynamic "play" of opposites, but the import of it is not the absolute triumph of either half. Things and beings and processes arise, they move, they are transformed, and they disappear. No conditionally apparent thing or being or process is ultimately preserved—nor, by contrast, is there any absolute destruction. Nature is a transformer—not merely a "creator" or a "destroyer".

To the ego (or present temporary form of being), self-preservation may seem to be the inevitable motive of being. Therefore, a struggle develops to destroy or escape the dynamic of conditional Nature by dominating "Evil" (or death) with "Good" (or immortality). This ideal gets expressed in the generally exoteric and Occidental (or more materialistic) efforts to conquer conditional Nature via worldly knowledge and power. However, it also gets expressed in the generally esoteric and Oriental (or more mystical) efforts to escape the plane of conditional Nature by ascent from materiality (or the "Evil" of the flesh) to "Heaven" (the "Good God" above the realm of conditional Nature).

When the ego (or self-contraction) is understood and transcended, then conditional Nature is seen from the "Point of View" of Wisdom. And, in that case, the egoic struggle in conditional Nature or against conditional Nature is also understood and transcended. Then life ceases to be founded on the need to defeat the dynamic of conditional Nature via conventional knowledge, power, immortality, or mystical escape. The world is no longer conceived as a drama of warfare between "Good" and "Evil". The righteousness of the search for the "Good" as a means of self-preservation disappears along with the self-indulgent and self-destructive negativity of possession by "Evil". In place of this dilemma of opposites, an ego-transcending and world-transcending (or Nature-transcending) equanimity appears. In that equanimity, there is an inherent Self-Radiance that transcends the egoic dualities of "Good" and "Evil" (or the conventional polarities of the separate self in conditional Nature). That Self-Radiance is the Free Radiance of egoless Love. In that Free Radiance, energy and attention are inherently free from the ego-bond, self-contraction, or the "gravitational effect" of phenomenal self-awareness. Therefore, dynamic equanimity, or the free disposition of egoless Love (rather than the egoic disposition in the modes of "Good" or "Evil"), is the "window" through which Real (Acausal) God may be "seen" (or intuited)—not in the conventional mode of "Creator", the "Good", the "Other", or the "Heavenly Place", but as <u>the Real</u> (or Reality Itself), the Self-Evidently Divine Self-Condition of all-and-All.

The ultimate moment in the "play" of conditional Nature is not the moment of egoic success (or the temporary achievement of the apparently positive, or "Good", effect). The ultimate moment is beyond contradiction (or the dynamics of polarized opposites). It is the moment of equanimity, the still point (or "eye") in the midst of the wheel of Nature's motions and all the motivations of the born self. The Truth and Real Self-Condition of self and Nature is Revealed only in that equanimity—beyond all stress and bondage of energy and attention.

This disposition of equanimity (or free energy and attention) is basic to the sixth and seventh stages of life. In the sixth stage of life, the disposition of equanimity provides the functional base for the ultimate and final investigation of the ego and the dynamics of conditional Nature. However, it is only in the only-by-Me Revealed and Given seventh stage of life that Fundamental (and Inherently egoless) Equanimity is Inherent and Constant, expressing Prior (and Permanent) Divine Self-Realization.

It is in the only-by-Me Revealed and Given seventh stage of life that Real (Acausal) God, Truth, or Reality is directly Obvious, Prior to every trace of egoity, dilemma, and seeking. Therefore, it is in the only-by-Me Revealed and Given seventh stage of life that Real (Acausal) God is truly proclaimed—not in the conventional mode of "Creator" (or of "Good"), but as the Real (or Reality Itself).

Real (Acausal) God is the Transcendental, Inherently Spiritual, and Self-Evidently Divine Truth, Reality, Identity, and Self-Condition of egoic self and conditional Nature. In the only-by-Me Revealed and Given seventh stage of life, That is tacitly obvious—and there is not anything that must be escaped or embraced for the Happiness of Most Perfect Real-God-Realization to be actualized. It is Inherently So.

Therefore, the only-by-Me Revealed and Given Way of Adidam is not any egoic means for <u>attaining</u> Real-God-Realization. The Way is Real-God-Realization <u>Itself</u>—through ego-transcending reception of My Avataric Divine Spiritual Grace, Beyond all the methods of the first six stages of life.

Real (Acausal) God—or the Transcendental, Inherently Spiritual, Inherently egoless, and Self-Evidently Divine Reality (Prior to conditional self, conditional world, and the ego-bound conventions of religion and non-religion)—Is the One and Only Truth of Reality Itself, and the One and Only Way of Right Life and Perfect Realization.

THE CULTURALLY PRESCRIBED "GOD"-IDEA OF EXOTERIC RELIGION IS NOT THE DIVINE ITSELF BUT ONLY A CULTURAL (AND ENTIRELY CONDITIONAL) MEANS FOR TURNING TO THE DIVINE

In the Hindu cultural tradition, there is a great variety of forms of exoteric religious worship—each of which is centered around a particular culturally prescribed Divine image, idea, and mythology. That focus of worship (however conceived, in any particular branch of the Hindu tradition) is regarded as one's "Chosen Form" of the One Divine Absolute. The understanding within the Hindu cultural tradition (in its most profound developments) is that whatever "Chosen Form" a person may worship (in the exoteric manner) is the construct through which he or she is moved to turn to the One Divine Absolute. Thus, it is understood that one's (exoterically worshipped) "Chosen Form" is not the One and Absolute Divine Itself, but is (rather) the culturally prescribed means whereby one turns to the One and Absolute Divine—because the One Divine Absolute Itself is (within the most profound developments of the Hindu cultural tradition) understood to transcend all constructs (and, altogether, all limiting conditions).

This understanding of the nature of exoteric religious worship is correct. Indeed, all the various modes of exoteric religion (not merely in India, but in all parts of the world and in all periods of history) should (rightly) be understood to be varietal forms (or variant possibilities) of (exoteric) devotion to a "Chosen Form" of the Divine—or to a particular culturally prescribed (and, in accordance with tradition, described) Divine image, idea, and mythology.

Westerners often (mistakenly) presume Hinduism to be (irreducibly) a form of polytheism (and, as such, of non-monotheism)—or the worship of many different (or separate) gods, rather than the worship of One God (or of the One Divine Absolute). However, the right understanding of the Hindu religious tradition is not that it allows for a great number of separate Absolute Divinities (or otherwise disallows the One Divine Absolute). Rather, the right understanding of the Hindu religious tradition is that it, without prejudice,

The Culturally Prescribed "God"-Idea of Exoteric Religion
Is Not the Divine Itself but Only a Cultural (and Entirely Conditional)
Means for Turning to the Divine

allows for the approach to the One Divine Absolute via (or by means of) any of the many possible "Chosen Forms" (or "Chosen-Form" traditions). The many different "Chosen Forms"—worshipped (in the exoteric manner) by different families or different local or regional cultures—are all presumed (within the Hindu cultural sphere) to be virtuous, because they are all understood to be means for turning to the Ultimate Divine (Which is everywhere understood to Be One, and to Be the Absolute and Only Reality).

The potential problem with conventional (exoteric) religious traditions (in general) is that any such tradition tends (or may tend) not to understand that its particular focus (or cult) of worship is simply one among many possible "Chosen Forms". Thus, any such tradition may tend to presume (or insist) that it is the tradition—the one and only true and right (and "officially" allowable) tradition. Such is the origin of fundamentalism. To the fundamentalist mind, the prescribed images (and the otherwise described ideas) of the cult define the Divine—as if the Divinity (or Reality Itself) has been "copyrighted", subject to exclusive "ownership" by a particular tradition of images and ideas.

When the exoteric traditions (themselves) thus replace the Divine (Itself) with their own contents, the result is (in effect) idolatry—which is what (characteristically) even the exoteric traditions themselves say should not be done. Rightly understood, the traditional admonitions against idolatry are not a matter of forbidding the worship (or worshipful use) of material images in temples. The "sin" of idolatry is any and every act (either personal or collective) of replacing the Divine Itself with the constructs of approach to the Divine.

All the exoteric religious traditions of the world—with their many and different images, ideas, and mythologies—are (each and all) true and right (insofar as they are, in fact, oriented to ego-surrendering worship of the Ultimate Divine, Which Is Reality Itself). But all exoteric religious traditions are themselves (in every sense of their nature and origin) constructs—whether a given tradition has, in the case of any individual, been inherited from one's family (or one's local, or regional, or national, or even international culture) or has been intentionally embraced (from among any number of studied or somehow experienced alternatives) in the course of one's life.

Ultimately, the process of truly maturing in religious life requires the transcending of <u>all</u> constructs. It is not that there must be no use of constructs whatsoever in one's approach to the Divine (or the One and Absolute Reality Itself). It is simply that all mere <u>constructs</u> must be understood to be <u>such</u> (and embraced <u>only</u> as such).

Ultimately, exoteric religion must become (or otherwise be superseded by) esoteric Spiritual practice—the ego-transcending, body-mind-transcending, construct-transcending process of entering (by esoteric—and, in due course, Perfect—Means) into That Which Is Inherently Beyond (and Prior to) <u>all</u> constructs and limitations.

The Three Great Principles of All Truth

I.   The Divine Principle of Indivisibility: Reality (Itself) is <u>Inherently</u> Indivisible (One and Divine and Non-conditional and Absolute)

II.   The Universal (or Cosmic) Principle of Unity and Non-"Difference": The world (or the conditionally manifested cosmos) is <u>Inherently</u> a Unity (Which, in and <u>As</u> its True Self-Condition, is <u>Inherently</u> Non-"different" from the One and Indivisible and Absolute and Non-conditional Divine Reality)

III. The psycho-physical Principle of Non-Separateness: The individual psycho-physical entity is <u>Inherently</u> Non-separate from the world-Unity (or the Inherently Unified cosmic Totality, Which is Whole and Universal) and, also, <u>Inherently</u> Non-separate from the Inherently Indivisible Divine Reality (or the One and Conscious Light That <u>Is</u> the One and Only Self-Condition of all-and-All)

These Three Principles, Proposed by Me, are (Effectively) an Integrated Whole and Single Proposition. They (Together) Comprise the philosophical (and Reality-Based, and Reality-Realization-Based) Foundation for the Only-by-Me Revealed and Given Way of Adidam (Which is the One and Only by-Me-Revealed and by-Me-Given "Radical" Way of the Heart). And They are, also, the Right and True Basis (and the Right and True Measure) for the Correct (and, inevitably, intellectually Liberating) Evaluation of <u>any</u> and <u>all</u> possible propositions of philosophical import made (now, or in the future, or in any time and place at all) by any one (or any school or tradition) at all.

REAL (ACAUSAL) GOD
IS THE DEEP OF THE WORLD

1. "Consider" This: True Religion (or The Real Spiritual, Transcendental, and Divine Way Of Life) Begins With The <u>Transcending</u> Of Awe and Wonder. Conditional Existence Naturally Evokes Awe and Wonder (and Even Terrible Fear and Stark Bewilderment), but True Religion (or The Real Spiritual, Transcendental, and Divine Way Of Life) Begins With The <u>Free</u> (and Really ego-Transcending) <u>Heart-Response</u> To What Is (<u>Otherwise</u>) Awesome and Wonderful.

Therefore, True (and, Necessarily, <u>Esoteric</u>—or Non-conventional, and Non-egoic) Religion Does Not Begin With a <u>belief</u> (or An ego-Based, and ego-Serving, Presumption) About "God". It Begins When You Truly (and Most Fundamentally) Understand (and Feel Beyond) the egoic self-Contraction Of The Heart (or The Sometimes believing, and Sometimes disbelieving, and Always self-Protective, and Always self-Defining, and Always self-limiting Recoil Of the body-mind From the Apparently Impersonal and Loveless forces Of conditional Nature).

2. Real (Acausal) God Is Obvious To The Free (or <u>egoless</u>) Heart. Only The Heart (Free Of self-Contraction) Can "Locate" (or See) and Realize The True and Real Acausal Divine Person.

The conditional (or self-Contracted) Heart Does Not Realize Real (Acausal) God In the present—and, Therefore, the Heartless body and the Heartless mind Become Pre-occupied With Seeking For ego-Fulfillment, ego-Release, and ego-Consolation, Through every kind of conditionally Attainable experience, knowledge, and belief (including merely conventional—or exoteric, or ego-Based, or "subject-object"-Based—Religious beliefs and practices).

3. Only Reality <u>Is</u> Real (Acausal) God.
Reality <u>Is</u>, Necessarily, Truth.
Only Truth <u>Is</u> Real (Acausal) God.
Real (Acausal) God <u>Is</u> Reality and Truth.

Real (Acausal) God <u>Is</u> The God Of Reality and Truth.

Real (Acausal) God <u>Is</u> The God That <u>Is</u> Reality and Truth.

Reality and Truth <u>Is</u> That Which Is Always Already The Case.

Real (Acausal) God <u>Is</u> That Which Is Always Already The Case.

Therefore, Real (Acausal) God Need Not Be Sought.

4. Real (Acausal) God Is Only <u>Avoided</u> By <u>Any</u> Kind Of Seeking.

To Seek Is To Fail To Admit and To Realize Real (Acausal) God, or That Which Is Always Already The Case.

Real (Acausal) God Is Realized Only By "Locating" That Which Is Always Already The Case.

5. Real (Acausal) God Is Not Other, Separate, or "Different". Real (Acausal) God (or The Acausal Divine Person—Which <u>Is</u> Reality, or Truth, or That Which Is Always Already The Case) Is Always Already (Inherently and Inherently Perfectly) Prior To The "Who", The "What", The "That", The "Where", The "When", The "How", and The "Why" That Is (By conditional experience, or conditional knowledge, or conditional belief) Presumed To Be Really and Only Other, Separate, or "Different". Therefore, Real (Acausal) God Is Always Already Prior To the ego-"I". Indeed, Real (Acausal) God Is Always Already Prior To each and every conditionally Attained experience, or form of knowledge, or form of belief.

6. Reality (Itself) <u>Is</u> The Only <u>Real</u> (Acausal) God.

7. Real (Acausal) God Is Not <u>The</u> <u>Maker</u> Of conditional Nature.

Real (Acausal) God Is <u>The</u> <u>Non-conditional</u> <u>Nature</u> (or Most Prior Condition) Of conditional Nature.

8. Real (Acausal) God Is Not Merely <u>The</u> <u>Cause</u> Of all causes and all effects.

Real (Acausal) God Is <u>The</u> <u>Source</u> and <u>The</u> <u>Source-Condition</u> Of all causes and all effects.

9. Real (Acausal) God Is Not The <u>Objective</u> Source and Source-Condition Of all causes and all effects.

Real (Acausal) God Is The (Perfectly) <u>Subjective</u> Source and Source-Condition (or Self-Condition) Of all causes and all effects.

10. Real (Acausal) God Is <u>Not</u> Inside (or Within) The self-Contracted Knot Of ego-"I".

Real (Acausal) God Is Always <u>Outside</u> The self-Contracted Knot Of ego-"I".

11. When You Transcend the self-Contraction (and The Knot) Of ego-"I", You Are Free In Real (Acausal) God.

When There Is <u>No</u> ego-"I"—Real (Acausal) God Is Not <u>Outside</u> You.

When There Is <u>No</u> ego-"I"—Real (Acausal) God Is Not <u>Within</u> You.

When There Is <u>No</u> ego-"I"—Real (Acausal) God <u>Is</u> You (Perfectly Prior To Your Apparently objective conditional self, and Perfectly Prior To Your Apparently subjective conditional self, and, Therefore, Perfectly Prior To Your Total, Complex, and Merely Apparent conditional self).

12. The conditional self and the worlds of the conditional self Are Not Created By Real (Acausal) God, Nor Were (or Are) the conditional self (itself) and the worlds of the conditional self (themselves) Perfect Originally, Nor Will (or Can) It Ever Be The Case That Real (Acausal) God (or, Otherwise, the conditional self, itself, or the worlds of the conditional self, themselves) Will Perfect the conditional self (itself) or

the worlds of the conditional self (themselves). But Only Real (Acausal) God (or Reality, or Truth, or That Which Is Always Already The Case) Is Perfect, For Real (Acausal) God (or Reality, or Truth, or That Which Is Always Already The Case) Is Perfection (or The Perfect Itself).

13. Therefore, the conditional self and the worlds of the conditional self May Evolve conditionally, but Only To Possible conditional Degrees (Forever Less Than Perfection Itself, Which Is The Condition Only Of Real Acausal God), and This Through The Struggle Made By The Submission Of the lesser (or the lower) imperfect (or the lesser, or the lower, conditional) To the greater (or the higher) imperfect (or the greater, or the higher, conditional). And the conditional self and the worlds of the conditional self May, Otherwise, Devolve conditionally, but Also Only To Possible conditional Degrees (and Never To The Degree Of Absolute, or Irreversible, or More Than Illusory Separation From Real Acausal God, or From The Perfect Itself, Which Is Real Acausal God), and This Through The Struggle Made By The Submission Of the greater (or the higher) or the lesser (or the lower) imperfect (or the greater, or the higher, or the lesser, or the lower, conditional) To the even lesser (or the even lower) forms of the imperfect (or the conditional) itself.

14. Nevertheless, and Whatever The (Relatively Evolved, or Relatively Devolved) Case May Be, The Only Way To Realize Real (Acausal) God (or The Transcendental, and Perfectly Subjective, and Inherently Spiritual, and Inherently egoless, and Inherently Perfect, and Self-Evidently Divine Self-Condition, and Source-Condition, Itself) Is To Progressively (or, However, Utterly) Surrender the imperfect itself (or the conditional self, and the worlds of the conditional self) To and Into Real (Acausal) God (or The Very, and Only, and Transcendental, and Perfectly Subjective, and Inherently

Spiritual, and Inherently egoless, and Inherently Perfect, and
Self-Evidently Divine Person, or Self-Condition, or Source-
Condition, That Is Real Acausal God), and, Most Ultimately
(and Inherently, and Inherently Most Perfectly), To
Transcend the imperfect (or the conditional self and the
worlds of the conditional self) In (and By Inherent, and
Inherently Most Perfect, and Perfectly Subjective Self-
Identification With) The Very, and Only, and Transcendental,
and Perfectly Subjective, and Inherently Spiritual, and
Inherently egoless, and Inherently Perfect, and Self-Evidently
Divine Person (or Self-Condition, or Source-Condition) That
Is Real (Acausal) God.

15. Even Though Real (Acausal) God (As Real Acausal God)
Merely Is (Always Already, or Inherently and Eternally Prior
To cause and effect), the "God"-Seeking ego-"I" (or every
human being whose Heart is self-Contracted, and who, As A
Result, Wants Toward "Ultimate" experience, knowledge, or
belief) Characteristically Tries To Argue For experience Of,
or knowledge Of, or belief In "God" (or The "Ultimate"
Proposed To Be experienced, known, or believed In) By
Appealing To The Logic Of cause and effect.

Therefore, In their "Ultimate" Arguments For The
"Ultimate", and In their (Necessarily, conditional) experiences, knowings, and believings Attained In The Course Of
their Seeking For The "Ultimate", the "God"-Seeking human
egos Propose That "God" Is The Cause (and The "Doer") Of
everything—but, Even Though they (Necessarily, conditionally) experience, or know, or believe, these (Necessarily,
conditionally) experiencing, or knowing, or believing egos
Do Not Stand Free. They Only Cling To the (Necessarily,
imperfect) conditional self and the (Necessarily, imperfect)
worlds of the conditional self.

Therefore, they Do Not Realize Real (Acausal) God (or
The Perfect, Itself) By Heart, Through ego-Transcending

Love-Communion, To The Inherently Most Perfect Degree
Of Inherently Perfect Love-Bliss (Beyond All "Difference").

16. Real (Acausal) God Is Not The Creator.
Real (Acausal) God Is The Liberator.
Real (Acausal) God Is Not The Way In.
Real (Acausal) God Is The Way Out.
The Way Of Real (Acausal) God
Is Not The Way Of
self-Seeking,
self-Increase, and
self-Success.
The Way Of Real (Acausal) God
Is The Way Of self-Sacrifice
(or ego-Transcendence).

17. Therefore, The Only-By-Me Revealed and Given "Radical"
Way Of The Heart (or Way Of Adidam) Is The Great Process
Of Devotional self-Sacrifice In Real (Acausal) God (By
Means Of ego-Surrendering, ego-Forgetting, and, Always
More and More, ego-Transcending Heart-Communion With
My Real-God-Revealing Avatarically-Born Bodily Human
Divine Form, My Avatarically Self-Transmitted Spiritual, and
Always Blessing, Divine Presence, and My Avatarically Self-
Revealed, and Very, and Transcendental, and Perfectly
Subjective, and Inherently Spiritual, and Inherently egoless,
and Inherently Perfect, and Self-Evidently Divine State). And,
By Means Of This Great Process, the Total psycho-physical
self Of My Devotee Is Surrendered To The Progressive
Course Of (Most Ultimately, Inherent, and Inherently Most
Perfect) Divine Self-Realization.

18. Real (Acausal) God Is The One and Only and Self-
Existing and Self-Radiant Conscious Light That Is Reality
(Itself).

63

Real (Acausal) God Is The God (or The Truth, The Reality, and The Self-Identity) Of Consciousness Itself.

19. Real (Acausal) God Is The God (or The Truth, The Reality, and The Self-Identity) Of Inherently Perfect Subjectivity.

Real (Acausal) God Is Not The "God" (or The Implicated Maker) Of conditional Nature, Separate self, and All Objectivity.

20. Real (Acausal) God Is The God (or The Truth and The Reality) Of Consciousness, Freedom, Love-Bliss, Being, and Oneness.

Real (Acausal) God Is Not The "God" (The Cause, The "Doer", or Even The Victim) Of Un-Consciousness (or mere causes and effects).

Therefore, Real (Acausal) God Is Not The "God" Of Bondage, Un-Happiness, Death (or Separation), and "Difference".

21. Real (Acausal) God Is The "Subject"—Not The Object.

Real (Acausal) God Is The Inherent Unity Of Being.

Real (Acausal) God Is The Integrity—Not The Cause—Of the world.

22. Real (Acausal) God Is The True Source, The Very Context, The Real "Substance", The Truth-Condition, The Very Reality, The Most Prior Condition, and The Eternal "Bright" Spherical Self-Domain Of all conditions, all causes, and all effects—For all that appears Comes From Real (Acausal) God (but In Real Acausal God, and Only As Real Acausal God).

23. All "things" Are the media of all "things", but Real (Acausal) God Is Not The Maker—For Real (Acausal) God Is Like A Hidden Spring Within the water's world, and Real

(Acausal) God Is Prior Even To Cause (and every cause), and Real (Acausal) God Is The Self-Domain Of Even every effect, and Real (Acausal) God Is The Being (Itself) Of all that appears.

Therefore, Real (Acausal) God Merely Is—and Is Is What Grants every appearance (every being, every thing, every condition, and every conditional process) The Divine Sign Of Mystery, Love, Bliss, and Joy.

24. Yes, Real (Acausal) God Is The Deep Of the world, and The Heart Of every Would-Be "I".

TRUE (OR REAL, OR ESOTERIC) RELIGION IS FOUNDED ON THE <u>DIRECT</u> <u>EXPERIENTIAL</u> <u>KNOWLEDGE</u> OF REALITY

I.

True (or Real, or esoteric) religion is <u>not</u> a matter of conventional "God"-ideas.

True (or Real, or esoteric) religion is <u>not</u> a matter of systematized beliefs.

True (or Real, or esoteric) religion is <u>not</u> a matter of hopeful mythologies.

True (or Real, or esoteric) religion is <u>not</u> a matter of preoccupation with visionary (or even hallucinatory) experience.

Conventional "God"-ideas, systematized beliefs, hopeful mythologies, and visionary experiences are <u>mind-forms</u>.

All mind-forms are <u>forms</u> of <u>mind</u>.

That is to say, all mind-forms are conditional manifestations.

Therefore, no mind-form is Truth Itself.

All notions that conventional "God"-ideas or systematized beliefs or hopeful mythologies or visionary experiences constitute Truth are rightly to be criticized—because they are <u>not</u> Truth.

However, such criticism is <u>not</u> a criticism of True (or Real, or esoteric) religion.

Rather, such criticism is a criticism of conventional (or popular, or exoteric) religion.

And conventional (or exoteric, or popular) religion is an entirely different kind of endeavor than True (or Real, or esoteric) religion.

Conventional (or popular, or exoteric) religion is founded on the allegiance to a particular (culturally and historically determined) collection of <u>mind-forms</u>.

True (or Real, or esoteric) religion is founded on the <u>direct</u> <u>experiential</u> <u>knowledge</u> of Reality (in all Its dimensions—not merely Its gross, or physical, dimension).

Conventional (or popular, or exoteric) religion requires a <u>commitment</u> to (one or another variety of) false views.

True (or Real, or esoteric) religion requires the utter <u>transcending</u> of <u>all</u> false views.

Therefore, remember this:

There is no mind-form that is Truth Itself.

There is no kind of commitment-to-mind-forms that is True (or Real, or esoteric) religion.

No criticism of any kind of commitment-to-mind-forms is a criticism of True (or Real, or esoteric) religion.

II.

In the "modern" West, the findings of science are often presumed, especially by those deeply involved in (or sympathetic with) the scientific endeavor, to have undermined the (historically inherited) absolute propositions of conventional (or exoteric) religion. However, both conventional religion <u>and</u> the philosophy of scientific materialism (which seeks to criticize conventional religion as if conventional religion were the <u>totality</u> of religion and Spirituality) are characteristic (and characteristically limited) "products" of the Omega "point of view". Science (itself) is simply a method for the free investigation of the phenomena of conditionally manifested existence—but science (itself) tends to be overlaid with the (traditional and ancient) philosophy of materialism, which philosophy is very much a part of the gross-minded Omega culture of the West.

The scientific examination of conditional phenomena has resulted in (and continues to pursue) the detailed mapping of the mechanisms of conditionally manifested existence, including much detailed knowledge about the functioning human organism and about the development of various modes of conditionally manifested life on Earth. (Of course, conventional religionists—in the attempt to defend their "creationist" mythologies—propagandize <u>against</u> evolutionary theories, and other scientifically proposed explanations that seem to contradict the traditionally held views of conventional religion.) Equipped with such maps of the structures of the human entity, proponents of scientific materialism have criticized many of the traditionally acknowledged means of accounting for human experience (including religious experience), claiming that conscious experience amounts to nothing more than evidence of how the human brain and the extended human body are "built" to function. According to this scientific materialist "point of view", religious experience (and all of human experience) is merely something happening in the "meat-organism", determined by its presumed-to-be-separate and fundamentally <u>physical</u> structuring. That conclusion regarding the nature of human experience is the superimposition of scientific materialist philosophy on the legitimate observations made by means of the scientific method. And that conclusion regarding the nature of human experience is a key fault, which makes scientific materialism a <u>false</u> philosophy.

The physical structures of the human mechanism do, in fact, pattern human experience and human behavior, including scientific behavior—and the <u>entire</u> psycho-physical range of potential human experience (only a fraction of which has been investigated by the efforts of conventional science) can be understood in terms of My "Map" of the seven stages of life, by means of which I have Revealed how <u>all</u> potential human developments are intrinsically related to the various (hierarchically interrelated) structures of the human <u>psycho-</u>physical (and not <u>exclusively</u> physical) mechanism. And, indeed, the findings of esoteric Yogic investigation are <u>entirely</u> <u>compatible</u> with what may be observed about the structure of the human entity by means of the scientific method (which is still, in the "modern" era, very much "in process" relative to its attempt to discover explanations for the complex realities of human experience). However, the scientific materialist "point of view" <u>reduces</u> everything to observable physical structures—as if (for example) the association between human religious experience and certain structures in the human brain proves that religion is <u>nothing but</u> a "side-effect" of the functioning of the brain.

Since the most ancient days, <u>all</u> esoteric traditions of Spirituality and Yoga have been associated with an understanding of the (real) structures underlying human experience. True Spirituality and true Yoga are based on a detailed knowledge of the cerebro-spinal system, of the various organs within the body, and so forth. True Spirituality and true Yoga are not based on (and, indeed, have nothing to do with) cosmological mythologies or the conventional "God"-ideas of popular religiosity. True esotericism is always associated with an analysis of the human structure, of the workings of that structure, and of the methods by which the esoteric practitioner can make use of that structure in the process of Realization. However, the esoteric traditions of Spirituality and Yoga are free of the fault of reductionism. In the esoteric traditions of Spirituality and Yoga, there is no notion that the association of religious and Spiritual experiential phenomena with certain aspects of the human structure reduces the significance of those experiential phenomena to nothing but the workings of that structure.

Through the entire collective human process of examining the nature of conditionally manifested existence (including the scientific examination of the development of life-forms on Earth, the origin and evolution of the universe, and so on), a single great principle is made evident: <u>All</u> manifestation is arising from a Prior and inherently Indivisible <u>Unity</u>. Everything that appears is developed from What is already <u>there</u>, inherently and potentially. That Prior Unity is fundamental to the Nature of Reality. Therefore, it is false philosophy to presume (or even insist) that Reality <u>Itself</u> is reducible to the observable "facts" of the presumed-to-be-separate human structure and its functioning.

This must be understood: The human psycho-physical structure is (irreducibly) part of the Prior and Universal Unity. Reality is Non-Separate, Indivisible, and (Ultimately) One—Beyond all appearances. The human psycho-physical structure is the "equipment" that is to be used by human beings for the sake of (Ultimately, Most Perfect) Divine Self-Realization—and that structure arises within the Universal Unity. This is the ancient esoteric knowledge.

III.

Although the esoteric traditions of Spirituality and Yoga acknowledge the significance of the human psycho-physical structure as the conditionally manifested mechanism by means of which the process of Realization is exercised, those traditions also exhibit the (characteristic) Alpha disposition of dissociation relative to the human psycho-physical structure (and relative to conditionally manifested existence altogether—or at least relative to the gross dimension of conditionally manifested existence). However, I do not Call My devotees to any such dissociative disposition relative to their own psycho-physical structure (or relative to any aspect of conditionally manifested existence whatsoever). I do not Call My devotees to the strategy of excluding attention from the gross dimension of the human psycho-physical structure. Indeed, the only-by-Me Revealed and Given Way of Adidam is specifically not founded on an attitude of dissociation from the existential context of the human body-mind. The practice of the only-by-Me Revealed and Given Way of Adidam is founded in the transcending of the human psycho-physical structure—but not by means of a dissociative act. Thus, the fundamental (and necessary) basis for the practice of the only-by-Me Revealed and Given Way of Adidam—which is the Way of the devotional and (in due course) Spiritual relationship to Me—is equanimity relative to one's own psycho-physical structure and relative to the psycho-physical context of human (and cosmic) existence.

When a <u>perceptually</u>-based and (in due course, through the reception of My Ruchira Shaktipat) <u>Spiritually</u>-based equanimity is established, the human psycho-physical structure is (thereby) truly and really made into a vehicle for the Divine Spiritual Process. Such is the true and real transcending of the fault of gross-minded philosophy (according to which philosophy the structures of the human body-mind are to be understood reductively as separate "somethings", and all religious and Spiritual experiences are regarded as merely aspects of a mortal physicality). Such perceptually-based and Spiritually-based equanimity makes it possible for My devotee to rightly understand (and relate to) his or her own body-mind—without falling into either the gross-minded Omega error of reductionism or the Alpha error of dissociation—as a manifestation arising within the context of a Universal Unity of utter Non-Separateness and Ultimate Non-"Difference". Thus established in the disposition of perceptually-based and (in due course) Spiritually-based equanimity, the body-mind of My devotee <u>participates</u> in That Which Is Universal, One, and (Ultimately) Beyond all conditions. In that participatory mode, the body-mind of My devotee <u>coincides</u> with That Which Is Universal, Spiritually Real, Transcendental, inherently egoless, and Self-Evidently Divine.

I have accounted for <u>all</u> aspects of potential human experience that arise out of the Prior and Universal Unity— from the grossest experiences of the first stage of life to the Ultimacy-Beyond-Ultimacy of the only-by-Me Revealed and Given seventh stage of life—and I have done so on the basis of My <u>direct</u> Awareness of the different structures that come into play in each stage of life (or mode of development).

I Stand entirely Apart from the conventional "God"-ideas and conventional mythologies of exoteric religion. I am Communicating an <u>Esoteric</u> Way—and, therefore, the only-by-Me

Revealed and Given Way of Adidam is the Completion and Fulfillment of the ancient tradition of (always <u>Reality</u>-based) esoteric Spirituality and Yoga. I Say (and have always Said) to you: <u>Reality</u> <u>Itself</u> <u>Is</u> <u>the</u> <u>Only</u> <u>Real</u> (<u>Acausal</u>) <u>God</u>. Reality Itself (or Truth Itself) <u>Is</u> <u>What</u> there <u>Is</u> to Realize.

Therefore, in My Communication about Reality (and the Process of Realizing Reality), I am not "on the side" of exoteric religiosity, nor am I "on the side" of scientific materialism. I am not "on" any "side" whatsoever—because I am not in the position of mind (or of separate "point of view"). My Communication is a Direct Revelation of Reality Itself (or Truth Itself), Which Is Inherently Indivisible, Inherently Non-Separate, Inherently Non-conditional, Intrinsically Self-Evident, and Self-Evidently Divine. The Process of Realizing Reality Itself (or Truth Itself) is (inevitably) related to the structures of the human being, and to the structures of conditionally manifested existence (altogether)—but that Process is (Ultimately) a matter of Perfectly (or Non-conditionally) Realizing That Which <u>Transcends</u> all such conditional structures, and (indeed) <u>all</u> of conditionally manifested existence (itself).

Thus, in Making My Revelation about Reality (and the process of Realizing Reality), I am not merely Communicating a philosophy. Rather, I am Revealing <u>Myself</u>. <u>This</u>—My Avatarically Self-Given Divine Self-Revelation—Is the Basis of the only-by-Me Revealed and Given Way of Adidam. Yes, My Avatarically Self-Revealed Divine Teaching-Word Accounts for <u>all</u> aspects of Reality, both conditional and Non-conditional. But, most fundamentally, My Avatarically Self-Revealed Divine Teaching-Word Accounts for <u>Myself</u>—and, in so doing, Accounts for the by-Me-Revealed and by-Me-Given Way of the devotional and (in due course) Spiritual relationship to Me.

Adidam—In January 1996, when Avatar Adi Da Samraj first Gave the name "Adidam" to the Way He has Revealed, He pointed out that the final "m" adds a mantric force, evoking the effect of the primal Sanskrit syllable "Om". (For Avatar Adi Da's Revelation of the most profound esoteric significance of "Om" as the Divine Sound of His own Very Being, see *The Dawn Horse Testament*.) Simultaneously, the final "m" suggests the English word "Am" (expressing "I Am"), such that the name "Adidam" also evokes Avatar Adi Da's Primal Self-Confession, "I Am Adi Da", or, more simply, "I Am Da" (or, in Sanskrit, "Aham Da Asmi").

Alpha and Omega—Avatar Adi Da calls the characteristic traditional Eastern strategy the "Alpha" strategy. Alpha cultures pursue an undisturbed peace, in which the conditional world is excluded as much as possible from attention (and thereby ceases to be a disturbance). Although the cultures that were originally founded on the Alpha approach to life and Truth are fast disappearing, the Alpha strategy remains the conventional archetype of Spiritual life, even in the Omega culture. In contrast to the Omega preference, the Alpha preference is to limit and control (and even suppress) attention to the conditional reality, while maximizing attention to the Divine Reality.

Avatar Adi Da uses the term "Omega" to characterize the materialistic culture that today dominates not only the Western world (which has brought the Omega strategy to its fullest development), but even most of the present-day Eastern world, which has now largely adopted the anti-Spiritual viewpoint typical of the West. The Omega strategy is motivated to the attainment of a future-time perfection and fulfillment of the conditional worlds, through the intense application of human invention, political will, and even Divine Influence. Its preference is to limit and suppress attention to the Divine Reality, while maximizing attention to the conditional reality.

Neither the Alpha strategy nor the Omega strategy Realizes Truth absolutely, as each is rooted in the presumption of a "problem" relative to existence. (For Avatar Adi Da's extended discussion of the Alpha and Omega strategies, see *The Truly Human New World-Culture Of Unbroken Real-God-Man*.)

"Bright"—By the word "Bright" (and its variations, such as "Brightness"), Avatar Adi Da refers to the Self-Existing and Self-Radiant Divine Reality that He has Revealed since His Birth. Avatar Adi Da Named His own Self-Evidently Divine Self-Condition "the 'Bright'" in His Infancy, as soon as He acquired the capability of language.

This term is placed in quotation marks to indicate that Avatar Adi Da uses it with the specific meaning described here.

"Bright" Spherical Self-Domain—*See* **Self-Domain, Divine "Bright" Spherical.**

"create" / "Creator"—Avatar Adi Da Samraj places the word "create" (and its variants) in quotation marks when He wishes to indicate the sense of "so to speak"—Communicating that, in the Indivisible Unity of Reality, any particular "thing" is not truly (but only apparently) appearing "out of nothing" or being caused to appear (or "created").

"difference"—The root of the egoic presumption of separateness—in contrast with the Realization of Oneness, or Non-"Difference", Which is Native to the Divine Acausal Self-Condition. This term is placed in quotation marks to indicate that Avatar Adi Da uses it in the "so to speak" sense. He is Communicating (by means of the quotation marks) that, in Reality, there is no such thing as "difference", even though it appears to be the case from the "point of view" of ordinary human perception.

ego-"I"—The fundamental activity of self-contraction, or the presumption of separate and separative existence.

The "I" is placed in quotation marks to indicate that it is used by Avatar Adi Da in the "so to speak" sense. He is Communicating (by means of the quotation marks) that, in Reality, there is no such thing as the separate "I", even though it appears to be the case

from the "point of view" of ordinary human perception.

Great Tradition—The "Great Tradition" is Avatar Adi Da's term for the total inheritance of human, cultural, religious, magical, mystical, Spiritual, and Transcendental paths, philosophies, and testimonies, from all the eras and cultures of humanity—which inheritance has (in the present era of worldwide communication) become the common legacy of humankind. The Way of Adidam is the Divine Way in Which the entire Great Tradition of humankind is at once culminated and transcended.

"late-time" (or "dark" epoch)—Avatar Adi Da uses the terms "late-time" and "'dark' epoch" to describe the present era—in which doubt of God (and of anything at all beyond mortal existence) is more and more pervading the entire world, and the self-interest of the separate individual is more and more regarded to be the ultimate principle of life.

These terms include quotation marks to indicate that they are used by Avatar Adi Da in the "so to speak" sense. In this case, He is Communicating (by means of the quotation marks) that, in Reality, the "darkness" of this apparent "late-time" is not Reality, or Truth, but only an appearance from the "point of view" of ordinary human perception.

"Locate"—To "Locate" Avatar Adi Da is to "Truly Heart-Find" Him. Avatar Adi Da places this term (and its variants) in quotation marks to indicate the sense of "so to speak"—because He is, in reality, Omnipresent, without any specific "location".

"missing the mark"—"Hamartia" (the word in New Testament Greek that was translated into English as "sin") was also an archery term meaning "missing the mark".

most fundamental self-understanding—A descriptive phrase for what Avatar Adi Da calls "hearing" Him. The devotee has begun to hear Avatar Adi Da when there is "most fundamental understanding" of the root-act of egoity (or self-contraction), or the unique capability to consistently transcend the self-contraction. The capability of true hearing is not something the ego can "achieve". That capability can only be Granted, by Means of Avatar Adi Da's Divine Spiritual Grace, to His devotee who has effectively completed the (eventually, Spiritually Awakened) process of listening (which is the beginner's process of the Way of Adidam).

Most Perfect / Most Ultimate—Avatar Adi Da uses the phrase "Most Perfect(ly)" in the sense of "Absolutely Perfect(ly)". Similarly, the phrase "Most Ultimate(ly)" is equivalent to "Absolutely Ultimate(ly)". "Most Perfect(ly)" and "Most Ultimate(ly)" are always references to the seventh (or Divinely Enlightened) stage of life. "Perfect(ly)" and "Ultimate(ly)" (without "Most") refer to the prac-

tice and Realization in the context of the "Perfect Practice" of the Way of Adidam (or, when Avatar Adi Da is making reference to the Great Tradition, to practice and Realization in the context of the sixth stage of life).

"Narcissus"—In Avatar Adi Da's Teaching-Revelation, "Narcissus" is a key symbol of the un-Enlightened individual as a self-obsessed seeker, enamored of his or her own self-image and egoic self-consciousness.

He is the ancient one visible in the Greek myth, who was the universally adored child of the gods, who rejected the loved-one and every form of love and relationship, and who was finally condemned to the contemplation of his own image—until, as a result of his own act and obstinacy, he suffered the fate of eternal separateness and died in infinite solitude.
—Avatar Adi Da Samraj
The Knee Of Listening

When Avatar Adi Da uses "Narcissus" as an archetypal reference to the activity of self-contraction, He places the name in quotation marks, to indicate that He is using the name metaphorically (rather than in reference to the character in the Greek myth). When He uses "Narcissus" in reference to the mythological character, the name is not placed in quotation marks. Avatar Adi Da uses the adjective "Narcissistic" in the sense of "relating to the activity of self-contraction", rather than in any more conventional meaning (particularly those meanings associated with the discipline of psychology).

Omega—*See* **Alpha and Omega.**

"Point of View" / "point of view"—In Avatar Adi Da's Wisdom-Teaching, "Point of View" is capitalized when referring to the "Position" of Consciousness Itself, Prior to (and independent of) the body-mind or conditional existence altogether. The "Point of View" of Consciousness Itself is the basis of the "Perfect Practice" of the Way of Adidam. Both terms are in quotation marks to indicate that Avatar Adi Da uses them in the "so to speak" sense. He is Communicating (by means of the quotation marks) that, in Reality, there is no such thing as a "point of view", even though it appears to be the case from the "point of view" of ordinary human perception.

"radical"—Derived from the Latin "radix", meaning "root". Thus, "radical" principally means "irreducible", "fundamental", or "relating to the origin". Thus, Avatar Adi Da defines "radical" as "at-the-root". Because Adi Da Samraj uses "radical" in this literal sense, it appears in quotation marks in His Wisdom-Teaching, in order to distinguish His usage from the common reference to an extreme (often political) view.

"Radical" Way of the Heart—The Way Avatar Adi Da Offers is the "Radical" Way of the Heart Itself, Which Is Real (Acausal) God, the Divine Self-Condition, the Divine Reality. He calls the Way of the Heart He has Revealed and Given "Radical", because it is always already "at-the-root", or Inherently Established in the Prior Condition of Reality Itself.

Real (Acausal) God—The True (and Perfectly Subjective) Source of all conditions, the True and Spiritual Divine Person—rather than any ego-made (and, thus, false, or limited) presumption about God.

Ruchira Shaktipat—The "Bright" (Ruchira) Spiritual Energy, or Spiritual Power (Shakti), of Ruchira Avatar Adi Da Samraj.

self-contraction—The fundamental presumption (and activity) of separation.

Self-Domain, Divine "Bright" Spherical—Avatar Adi Da affirms that there is a Divine Self-Domain that is the Perfectly Subjective Condition of the conditional worlds. It is not "elsewhere", not an objective "place" (like a subtle "heaven" or mythical "paradise"), but It is the Self-Evidently Divine Source-Condition of every conditionally manifested being and thing—and It is not other than Avatar Adi Da Himself. Avatar Adi Da Reveals that His Divine Self-Domain is a Boundless (and Boundlessly "Bright") Sphere. To Realize the seventh stage of life (by the Divine Spiritual Grace of Avatar Adi Da Samraj) is to Awaken to His Divine Self-Domain. See *The Dawn Horse Testament*.

sin—*See* **"missing the mark"**.

stages of life—Avatar Adi Da
Samraj describes the potential
experiences and Realizations of
humankind in terms of seven
stages of life. This schema is one
of Avatar Adi Da's unique Gifts to
humanity—His precise "mapping"
of the potential developmental
course of human experience as it
unfolds through the gross, subtle,
and causal dimensions of the
being. He describes this course in
terms of six stages of life—which
account for, and correspond to, all
possible orientations to Reality (both
conditional and Non-conditional)
that have arisen in human history.
His own Avataric Divine Self-
Revelation—the Realization of the
"Bright", Prior to all experience—is
the seventh stage of life.
Understanding this structure of
seven stages illuminates the
unique nature of Avatar Adi Da's
"Sadhana Years" (and of the
Spiritual process in His Company).
See booklet one of the "Perfect
Knowledge" series for a full
description.

**Tacit Self-Apprehension of
Being**—The uncaused, unquali-
fied, direct, and wordless intuition
of the Self-Evidently Divine Self-
Condition.

The Avataric Great Sage,
ADI DA SAMRAJ

Become a Formal Devotee of Avatar Adi Da Samraj

In the depth of every human being, there is a profound need for answers to the fundamental questions of existence. Is there a God? What is beyond this life? Why is there suffering? What is Truth? What is Reality?

In this book, you have been introduced to the Wisdom-Revelation of Avatar Adi Da, whose Teachings truly and completely address all of these fundamental questions. How can Avatar Adi Da resolve these fundamental questions? Because He speaks, not from the "point of view" of the human dilemma, but directly from the unique Freedom of His Divine State. Adi Da's Birth in 1939 was an intentional embrace of the human situation, for the sake of Revealing the Way of Divine Liberation to all and Offering the Spiritual Blessing that carries beings to that true Freedom. He is thus the fulfillment of the ancient intuitions of the "Avatar"—the One Who Appears in human Form, as a direct manifestation of the Unmanifest Reality.

Through a 28-year process of Teaching-Work (beginning in 1972), Avatar Adi Da established the Way of Adidam—the Way of the devotional and Spiritual relationship to Him. In those years of Teaching, He spoke for many hours with groups of His devotees—always looking for them, as representatives of humanity, to ask all of their questions about God, Truth, Reality, and human life. In response, He Gave the ecstatic Way of heart-Communion with Him, and all the details of how that process unfolds. Thus, He created a new tradition, based on His direct Revelation (as Avatar) of the Divine Reality.

Avatar Adi Da Samraj does not offer you a set of beliefs, or even a set of Spiritual techniques. He simply Offers you His Revelation of Truth as a Free Gift. If you are moved to take up His Way, He invites you to enter into an extraordinarily deep and transformative devotional and Spiritual relationship to Him. On the following pages, we present a number of ways that you can choose to deepen your response to Adi Da Samraj and consider becoming His formal devotee.

To find Avatar Adi Da Samraj is to find the Very Heart of Reality—tangibly felt in your own heart as the Deepest Truth of Existence. This is the great mystery that you are invited to discover. ∎

A didam is not a conventional religion.
Adidam is not a conventional way of life.
Adidam is about the transcending of the ego-"I".
Adidam is about the Freedom of Divine Self-Realization.

Adidam is not based on mythology or belief.
Adidam is a "reality practice".
Adidam is a "reality consideration", in which the various modes of egoity are progressively transcended.

Adidam is a universally applicable Way of life.
Adidam is for those who will choose It, and whose hearts and intelligence fully respond to Me and My Offering.
Adidam is a Great Revelation, and It is to be freely and openly communicated to all.

AVATAR ADI DA SAMRAJ

*For what you can do next to respond to Avatar Adi Da's
Offering, or to simply find out more about Him
and the Way of Adidam, please use the information
given in the following pages.*

**Contact an Adidam center near you
for courses and events**
(p. 86)

Visit our website: www.adidam.org
(p. 87)

**For young people:
Join the Adidam Youth Fellowship**
(p. 88)

**Support Avatar Adi Da's Work
and the Way of Adidam**
(p. 88)

**Order other books and recordings
by and about Avatar Adi Da Samraj**
(pp. 89–93)

Contact an Adidam center
near you

■ To find out about becoming a formal devotee of Avatar
Adi Da, and for information about upcoming courses,
events, and seminars in your area:

AMERICAS
12040 North Seigler Road
Middletown, CA 95461 USA
1-707-928-4936

PACIFIC-ASIA
12 Seibel Road
Henderson
Auckland 1008
New Zealand
64-9-838-9114

AUSTRALIA
P.O. Box 244
Kew 3101
Victoria
1800 ADIDAM
(1800-234-326)

EUROPE-AFRICA
Annendaalderweg 10
6105 AT Maria Hoop
The Netherlands
31 (0)20 468 1442

THE UNITED KINGDOM
uk@adidam.org
0845-330-1008

INDIA
Shree Love-Ananda Marg
Rampath, Shyam Nagar Extn.
Jaipur–302 019, India
91 (141) 2293080

E-MAIL:
correspondence@adidam.org

■ For more contact information about local Adidam
groups, please see **www.adidam.org/centers**

Visit our website:
www.adidam.org

■ **SEE AUDIO-VISUAL PRESENTATIONS** on the Divine Life and Spiritual Revelation of Avatar Adi Da Samraj

■ **LISTEN TO DISCOURSES** Given by Avatar Adi Da Samraj to His practicing devotees—
  ■ Transcending egoic notions of God
  ■ Why Reality cannot be grasped by the mind
  ■ How the devotional relationship to Avatar Adi Da moves you beyond ego-bondage
  ■ The supreme process of Spiritual Transmission

■ **READ QUOTATIONS** from the "Source-Texts" of Avatar Adi Da Samraj—
  ■ Real God as the <u>only</u> Reality
  ■ The ancient practice of Guru-devotion
  ■ The two opposing life-strategies characteristic of the West and the East—and the way beyond both
  ■ The Prior Unity at the root of all that exists
  ■ The limits of scientific materialism
  ■ The true religion beyond all seeking
  ■ The esoteric structure of the human being
  ■ The real process of death and reincarnation
  ■ The nature of Divine Enlightenment

■ **SUBSCRIBE** to the online *Adidam Revelation* magazine

For young people:
Join the Adidam Youth Fellowship

■ Young people under 21 can participate in the "Adidam Youth Fellowship"—either as a "friend" or practicing member. Adidam Youth Fellowship members participate in study programs, retreats, celebrations, and other events with other young people responding to Avatar Adi Da. To learn more about the Youth Fellowship, call or write:

Vision of Mulund Institute (VMI)
10336 Loch Lomond Road, PMB 146
Middletown, CA 95461
phone: (707) 928-6932
e-mail: vmi@adidam.org
www.visionofmulund.org

Support Avatar Adi Da's Work
and the Way of Adidam

■ If you are moved to serve Avatar Adi Da's Spiritual Work specifically through advocacy and/or financial patronage, please contact:

Advocacy
12180 Ridge Road
Middletown, CA 95461
phone: (707) 928-5267
e-mail: adidam_advocacy@adidam.org

Order other books and recordings by and about Avatar Adi Da Samraj

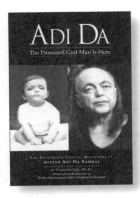

ADI DA

The Promised God-Man Is Here

The biography of Avatar Adi Da from His Birth to present time. Includes a wealth of quotations from His Writings and Talks, as well as stories told by His devotees. 358 pp., **$16.95**

ADIDAM

The True World-Religion Given by the Promised God-Man, Adi Da Samraj

A direct and simple summary of the fundamental aspects of the Way of Adidam. 196 pp., **$16.95**

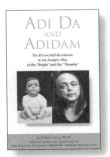

ADI DA AND ADIDAM

The Divine Self-Revelation of the Avataric Way of the "Bright" and the "Thumbs"

A brief introduction to Avatar Adi Da Samraj and His Unique Spiritual Revelation of the Way of Adidam. 64 pp., **$3.95**

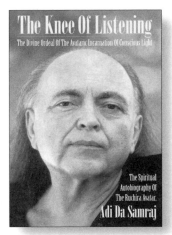

THE KNEE OF LISTENING

*The Divine Ordeal Of
The Avataric Incarnation
Of Conscious Light*

*The Spiritual Autobiography
Of The Ruchira Avatar,
Adi Da Samraj*

Born in 1939 on Long Island, New York, Adi Da Samraj describes His earliest life as an existence of constant and unmitigated Spiritual "Brightness". His observation, still in infancy, that others did not live in this manner led Him to undertake an awesome quest—to discover why human beings suffer and how they can transcend that suffering. His quest led Him to a confrontation with the bleak despair of post-industrial Godlessness, to a minute examination of the workings of subjective awareness, to discipleship in a lineage of profound Yogis, to a period of intense Christian mysticism, and finally to a Re-Awakening to the perfect state of "Brightness" He had known at birth.

In *The Knee Of Listening,* Avatar Adi Da also reveals His own direct awareness of His "deeper-personality vehicles"—the beings whose lives were the direct antecedents (or the "pre-history") of His present human lifetime—the great nineteenth-century Indian Realizers Sri Ramakrishna and Swami Vivekananda. Finally, Avatar Adi Da describes the series of profound transformational events that took place in the decades after His Divine Re-Awakening—each one a form of "Yogic death" for which there is no recorded precedent.

Altogether, *The Knee Of Listening* is the unparalleled history of how the Divine Conscious Light has Incarnated in human form, in order to grant everyone the possibility of Ultimate Divine Liberation, Freedom, and Happiness.

The Knee Of Listening *is without a doubt the most profound Spiritual autobiography of all time.*

—ROGER SAVOIE, PhD
philosopher; translator; author, *La Vipère et le Lion:
La Voie radicale de la Spiritualité*

822 pp., **$24.95**

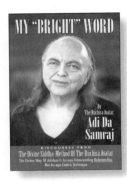

MY "BRIGHT" WORD

by Adi Da Samraj

New Edition of the Classic Spiritual Discourses originally published as *The Method of the Siddhas*

In these Talks from the early years of His Teaching-Work, Avatar Adi Da Gives extraordinary Instruction on the foundation of True Spiritual life, covering topics such as the primary mechanism by which we are preventing the Realization of Truth, the means to overcome this mechanism, and the true function of the Spiritual Master in relation to the devotee.

In modern language, this volume teaches the ancient all-time trans-egoic truths. It transforms the student by paradox and by example. Consciousness, understanding, and finally the awakened Self are the rewards. What more can anyone want?

—ELMER GREEN, PhD
Director Emeritus, Center for Applied Psychophysiology,
The Menninger Clinic

544 pp., **$24.95**

BUDDHISM, ADVAITISM, AND THE WAY OF ADIDAM

a Talk by Avatar Adi Da Samraj

Rather than being about egoity and seeking, the Way of Adidam is about the magnification of the understanding of egoity and its seeking. It is about a Revealed Process that directly transcends egoity in every moment, rather than merely at the end.

—AVATAR ADI DA SAMRAJ
June 21, 1995

In this remarkable Talk, Avatar Adi Da gives a unique summary of the ultimate Realizations in Buddhism and Advaitism (or Advaita Vedanta), and describes the sympathetic likenesses between these traditions and the Way of Adidam. Avatar Adi Da clarifies the uniqueness of the Way of Adidam, which is not based on strategically excluding conditional reality, but on transcending it.

CD, 5 Tracks, total running time: 55 minutes
$16.95

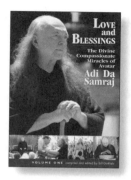

LOVE AND BLESSINGS

The Divine Compassionate Miracles of Avatar Adi Da Samraj

In *Love and Blessings—The Divine Compassionate Miracles of Avatar Adi Da Samraj*, twenty-five of His devotees tell heart-breaking stories of human need and Divine Response. A soldier in Iraq, a woman going blind in Holland, a son with his dying father in Australia, a woman with cancer in America—these and others tell how they asked Adi Da Samraj for His Blessing-Regard and the miraculous process that ensued.

248 pp., **$19.95**

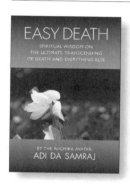

EASY DEATH

Spiritual Wisdom on the Ultimate Transcending of Death and Everything Else
by Adi Da Samraj

This new edition of *Easy Death* is thoroughly revised and updated with:

■ New Talks and Essays from Avatar Adi Da on death and ultimate transcendence

■ Accounts of profound Events of Yogic Death in Avatar Adi Da's own Life

■ Stories of His Blessing in the death transitions of His devotees

. . . an exciting, stimulating, and thought-provoking book that adds immensely to the ever-increasing literature on the phenomena of life and death. But, more important, perhaps, it is a confirmation that a life filled with love instead of fear can lead to ultimately meaningful life and death.

Thank you for this masterpiece.

—ELISABETH KÜBLER-ROSS, MD
author, *On Death and Dying*

544 pp., **$24.95**

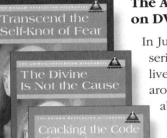

The Adidam Revelation Discourses on DVD

In July of 2004, Adi Da Samraj began a series of Discourses that were broadcast live over the internet to all His devotees around the world. During these remarkable occasions, Adi Da Samraj answered questions from those who were present in the room with Him, but also from devotees in other parts of the world via speakerphone. The "Adidam Revelation Discourse" DVDs offer you the opportunity to see and hear Avatar Adi Da speak in these unique and intimate occasions of Divine Instruction to His devotees. Current available titles include:

TRANSCEND THE SELF-KNOT OF FEAR

Running time: 60 minutes. Includes subtitles in English, Spanish, French, German, Dutch, and Polish.

THE DIVINE IS NOT THE CAUSE

Running time: 72 minutes. Includes subtitles in English, Spanish, French, German, Dutch, Finnish, Polish, Czech, Chinese, Japanese, and Hebrew.

CRACKING THE CODE OF EXPERIENCE

Running time: 86 minutes. Includes subtitles in English, Spanish, German, Dutch, Polish, Czech, Chinese, Japanese, and Hebrew.

DVD, **$26.95** each

To find out about and order other "Source-Texts", books, tapes, CDs, DVDs, and videos by and about Avatar Adi Da, contact your local Adidam regional center, or contact the Dawn Horse Press at:

1-877-770-0772 (from within North America)
1-707-928-6653 (from outside North America)
Or order online from: **www.dawnhorsepress.com**

The Five Books of the "Perfect Knowledge" Series

The books of the "Perfect Knowledge" Series are drawn from _Is:
The "Perfect Knowledge" of Reality and The "Radical" Way
to Realize It_, by the Avataric Great Sage, Adi Da Samraj.
The five books of the "Perfect Knowledge" Series together comprise
the complete text of _Is_.

THE PERFECT TRADITION

_The Wisdom-Way of the Ancient Sages
and Its Fulfillment in the Way of
"Perfect Knowledge"_

_by The Avataric Great Sage,
Adi Da Samraj_

RELIGION AND REALITY

_True Religion Is Not Belief in Any
"God"-Idea but the Direct Experiential
Realization of Reality Itself_

_by The Avataric Great Sage,
Adi Da Samraj_

THE LIBERATOR

_The "Radical" Reality-Teachings
of The Avataric Great Sage,
Adi Da Samraj_

**THE ANCIENT
REALITY-TEACHINGS**

_The Single Transcendental Truth
Taught by the Great Sages of
Buddhism and Advaitism—
As Revealed by
The Avataric Great Sage,
Adi Da Samraj_

**THE WAY OF
PERFECT KNOWLEDGE**

_The "Radical" Practice of
Transcendental Spirituality
in the Way of Adidam_

_by The Avataric Great Sage,
Adi Da Samraj_

The Avataric Divine Wisdom-Teaching
of Adi Da Samraj

The Avataric Divine Wisdom-Teaching of Adi Da Samraj is gathered together, in its final form, in the many "Source-Texts" which He has designated as His Eternal Communication to humankind. These "Source-Texts" are "True-Water-Bearers", or Bearers of the "True Water" of the "Bright" Divine Reality Itself.

Avatar Adi Da has grouped His "Source-Texts" into twenty-three "Streams", or "Courses". Each of these Courses conveys a particular aspect of His Avataric Divine Wisdom-Teaching—and each Course (other than the first) may, in principle, include any number of "Source-Texts".

The first Course is Avatar Adi Da's paramount "Source-Text", *The Dawn Horse Testament Of The Ruchira Avatar*. The remaining twenty-two Courses are divided into two groups: *The Heart Of The Adidam Revelation* (consisting of five Courses, which, together, present a comprehensive overview of Avatar Adi Da's entire Wisdom-Teaching) and *The Companions Of The True Dawn Horse* (consisting of seventeen Courses, each of which elaborates on particular topics from *The Dawn Horse Testament*).

> *The "Source-Texts"*
> *(or True-Water-Bearers)*
> *Of My Avataric Divine Wisdom-Teaching*
> *(In Its Twenty-Three Courses Of*
> *True-Water-Born Speech)—*
> *With [My] Divine Testament*
> *As The Epitome*
> *(or First and Principal Text,*
> *and "Bright" True-Water-Mill)*
> *Among Them—*
> *Are, Together, [My] Sufficient Word—*
> *Given, In Summary,*
> *To You*
> *(and, Therefore, To all).*
>
> —Avatar Adi Da Samraj
> *The Dawn Horse Testament*
> *Of The Ruchira Avatar*

The "Source-Texts" of the Avataric Divine Wisdom-Teaching of Adi Da Samraj (in Its Twenty-Three Courses)

The Dawn Horse Testament Of The Ruchira Avatar
(in Its Single Course)

THE DAWN HORSE TESTAMENT OF THE RUCHIRA AVATAR
*The Testament Of Divine Secrets Of The Divine World-Teacher,
Ruchira Avatar Adi Da Samraj*

The Heart Of The Adidam Revelation
(in Its Five Courses)

1. AHAM DA ASMI
   (BELOVED, I AM DA)
   *The "Late-Time" Avataric Revelation Of The True and Spiritual
   Divine Person (The egoless Personal Presence Of Reality and Truth,
   Which Is The Only Real Acausal God)*

2. RUCHIRA AVATARA GITA
   (THE AVATARIC WAY OF THE DIVINE HEART-MASTER)
   *The "Late-Time" Avataric Revelation Of The Great Secret Of The Divinely Self-
   Revealed Way That Most Perfectly Realizes The True and Spiritual Divine
   Person (The egoless Personal Presence Of Reality and Truth,
   Which Is The Only Real Acausal God)*

3. DA LOVE-ANANDA GITA
   (THE FREE AVATARIC GIFT OF THE DIVINE LOVE-BLISS)
   *The "Late-Time" Avataric Revelation Of The Great Means To Worship and
   To Realize The True and Spiritual Divine Person (The egoless Personal Presence
   Of Reality and Truth, Which Is The Only Real Acausal God)*

4. HRIDAYA ROSARY
   (FOUR THORNS OF HEART-INSTRUCTION)
   *The "Late-Time" Avataric Revelation Of The Universally Tangible Divine
   Spiritual Body, Which Is The Supreme Agent Of The Great Means To Worship
   and To Realize The True and Spiritual Divine Person (The egoless Personal
   Presence Of Reality and Truth, Which Is The Only Real Acausal God)*

5. ELEUTHERIOS
   (THE ONLY TRUTH THAT SETS THE HEART FREE)
   *The "Late-Time" Avataric Revelation Of The "Perfect Practice" Of The Great
   Means To Worship and To Realize The True and Spiritual Divine Person
   (The egoless Personal Presence Of Reality and Truth, Which Is The Only
   Real Acausal God)*

The Companions Of The True Dawn Horse
(in Their Seventeen Courses)

1. REAL (ACAUSAL) GOD IS THE INDIVISIBLE ONENESS OF UNBROKEN LIGHT
   Reality, Truth, and The "Non-Creator" God In The Universal Transcendental Spiritual Way Of Adidam

   THE TRANSMISSION OF DOUBT
   Transcending Scientific Materialism

2. THE TRULY HUMAN NEW WORLD-CULTURE OF UNBROKEN REAL-GOD-MAN
   The Eastern Versus The Western Traditional Cultures Of Humankind, and The Unique New Non-Dual Culture Of The Universal Transcendental Spiritual Way Of Adidam

   SCIENTIFIC PROOF OF THE EXISTENCE OF GOD WILL SOON BE ANNOUNCED BY THE WHITE HOUSE!
   Prophetic Wisdom about the Myths and Idols of Mass Culture and Popular Religious Cultism, the New Priesthood of Scientific and Political Materialism, and the Secrets of Enlightenment Hidden in the Human Body

   NOT-TWO IS PEACE
   The Ordinary People's Way of Global Cooperative Order

3. THE ONLY COMPLETE WAY TO REALIZE THE UNBROKEN LIGHT OF REAL (ACAUSAL) GOD
   An Introductory Overview Of The "Radical" Divine Way Of The Universal Transcendental Spiritual Way Of Adidam

4. THE KNEE OF LISTENING
   The Divine Ordeal Of The Avataric Incarnation Of Conscious Light— The Spiritual Autobiography Of The Avataric Great Sage, Adi Da Samraj

5. THE DIVINE SIDDHA-METHOD OF THE RUCHIRA AVATAR
   The Divine Way Of Adidam Is An ego-Transcending Relationship, Not An ego-Centric Technique

   Volume I: MY "BRIGHT" WORD

   Volume II: MY "BRIGHT" SIGHT

   Volume III: MY "BRIGHT" FORM

   Volume IV: MY "BRIGHT" ROOM

6. THE "FIRST ROOM" TRILOGY

BOOK ONE:
THE MUMMERY BOOK
A Parable Of Divine Tragedy, Told By Means Of
A Self-Illuminated Illustration Of The Totality Of Mind

BOOK TWO:
THE SCAPEGOAT BOOK
The Previously Secret Dialogue on the Avatarically Given Divine Way of
"Perfect-Knowledge"-Only, Once-Spoken in a Single Night of Conversation,
Between the Captive Divine Avatar and Great Sage, Raymond Darling, and
His Captor, the Great Fool, and False Teacher, and Notoriously Eccentric
Super-Criminal, Evelyn Disk—Herein Fully Given, Without Evelyn Disk's
Later and Famous and self-Serving Revisions, but Exactly As They Were
Originally Tape-Recorded, by Evelyn Disk himself, in the First Room, at the
State Mental Facility, near God's End, and Presented in Exact Accordance
with the Recent Revelatory and Complete Recounting, Given to the Waiting
World of Intelligent and Receptive Persons, by Meridian Smith, Who Was,
As Usual, Inexplicably Present

BOOK THREE:
THE HAPPENINE BOOK
The Childhood Teachings and The End-of-Childhood Revelations of The Famous
"Infant Sage", Raymond Darling—Compiled from Raymond Darling's
Original Handwritten Manuscripts, and Privately Held Tape-Recordings,
Discovered in The First Room By His True Servant-Devotee, Meridian Smith,
After The Miraculous Disappearance of The Avataric Great Sage

7. HE-AND-SHE IS ME
The Indivisibility Of Consciousness and Light In The Divine Body Of
The Ruchira Avatar

8. RUCHIRA SHAKTIPAT YOGA
The Divine (and Not Merely Cosmic) Spiritual Baptism In The Divine Way
Of Adidam

9. RUCHIRA TANTRA YOGA
The Physical-Spiritual (and Truly Religious) Method Of Mental, Emotional,
Sexual, and Whole Bodily Health and Enlightenment In The Divine Way
Of Adidam

EASY DEATH
Spiritual Wisdom on the Ultimate Transcending of Death and Everything Else

CONSCIOUS EXERCISE AND THE TRANSCENDENTAL SUN
The Universal ego-Transcending Principle of Love Applied to Exercise and
the Method of Common Physical Action—A Science of Whole Bodily Wisdom,
or True Emotion, Intended Most Especially for Those Engaged in Religious
(and, in Due Course, Spiritual) Life

THE EATING GORILLA COMES IN PEACE
The Universal ego-Transcending Principle of Love Applied to Diet and the Regenerative Discipline of True Health

LOVE OF THE TWO-ARMED FORM
The Practice of Right Regenerative Sexuality in Ordinary Life, and the Transcending of Sexuality in True Spiritual Practice

10. THE SEVEN STAGES OF LIFE
Transcending The Six Stages Of egoic Life, and Realizing The ego-Transcending Seventh Stage Of Life, In The Divine Way Of Adidam

11. THE ALL-COMPLETING AND FINAL DIVINE REVELATION TO HUMANKIND
A Summary Description Of The Supreme Yoga Of The Seventh Stage Of Life In The Divine Way Of Adidam

12. WHAT, WHERE, WHEN, HOW, WHY, AND WHO TO REMEMBER TO BE HAPPY
A Simple Explanation Of The Divine Way Of Adidam (For Children, and Everyone Else)

13. NO SEEKING / MERE BEHOLDING
The Always Primary Practice Of The Divine Way Of Adidam

14. SANTOSHA ADIDAM
The Essential Summary Of The Divine Way Of Adidam

15. THE LION SUTRA
The "Perfect Practice" Teachings In The Divine Way Of Adidam

16. THE OVERNIGHT REVELATION OF CONSCIOUS LIGHT
The "My House" Discourses On The Indivisible Tantra Of Adidam

17. THE BASKET OF TOLERANCE
The Perfect Guide To Perfectly Unified Understanding Of The One and Great Tradition Of Humankind, and Of The Divine Way Of Adidam As The Perfect Completing Of The One and Great Tradition Of Humankind

UP?
Beyond the Beginner's Spiritual Way of Saint Jesus and the Traditions of Mystical Cosmic Ascent via Spirit-Breath

IS
The "Perfect Knowledge" of Reality and The "Radical" Way to Realize It

NIRVANASARA
The Essence of the Teaching of Reality in the Realistic Traditions of Buddhism, in the Idealistic Traditions of Advaita Vedanta, and in the "Radical" World-Teaching of Adidam

We invite you to find out more about Avatar Adi Da Samraj and the Way of Adidam

■ Find out about our courses, seminars, events, and retreats by calling the regional center nearest you.

AMERICAS
12040 N. Seigler Rd.
Middletown, CA
95461 USA
1-707-928-4936

**THE UNITED
KINGDOM**
uk@adidam.org
0845-330-1008

EUROPE-AFRICA
Annendaalderweg 10
6105 AT Maria Hoop
The Netherlands
31 (0)20 468 1442

PACIFIC-ASIA
12 Seibel Road
Henderson
Auckland 1008
New Zealand
64-9-838-9114

AUSTRALIA
P.O. Box 244
Kew 3101
Victoria
**1800 ADIDAM
(1800-234-326)**

INDIA
Shree Love-Ananda Marg
Rampath, Shyam Nagar Extn.
Jaipur–302 019, India
91 (141) 2293080

E-MAIL: **correspondence@adidam.org**

■ Order books, tapes, CDs, DVDs, and videos by and about Avatar Adi Da Samraj.
1-877-770-0772 (from within North America)
1-707-928-6653 (from outside North America)
order online: **www.dawnhorsepress.com**

■ Visit us online:
www.adidam.org
Explore the online community of Adidam and discover more about Avatar Adi Da and the Way of Adidam.